PLAIN SPEAK MANAGEMENT

Can AI lead with empathy or inspire with passion?

As the world races ahead, chasing bigger dreams and tighter deadlines, management is no longer just about hitting targets or organizing workflows. It's about mastering the art of balancing humanity's heartbeat with the sharp edge of logic. It's the place where emotion meets strategy, and compassion becomes the driving force behind success.

In this philosophy lies the essence or what you may call the mantra of Ranjan Kumar Mohapatra, a thinker and believer who redefines management as the meeting point of human connection and intellectual clarity.

His book invites us to lead not with authority, but with authenticity, reminding us that the most effective managers are those who manage people, not just processes.

This book delves deep into how each thought from Ranjan Kumar Mohapatra resonates with the timeless lessons from iconic legends like Mahatma Gandhi, Nelson Mandela, Baji Rout, Bhima Bhoi or Albert Einstein. These extraordinary individuals transcended the limits of their times, offering lessons that remain as relevant today as they were decades ago. But why do their teachings endure in an age dominated by AI and rapid technological advancements? Because the essence of humanity; empathy, passion, and resilience; cannot possibly be automated.

Management thrives where machines end – at the human touch!

PLAIN SPEAK MANAGEMENT

Insights from Life's Lessons

Dr. Ranjan Kumar Mohapatra, Ph.D.

CONCEPT PUBLISHING COMPANY PVT. LTD.
NEW DELHI - 110 059

ISBN: 978-93-6344-536-9 (HB)
ISBN: 978-93-6344-684-7 (PB)

First Published 2025

Published and Printed by

Concept Publishing Company Pvt. Ltd.
A/15-16, Commercial Block, Mohan Garden
New Delhi-110059 (India)
T: +91-11-41101460
E: publishing@conceptpub.com, *W*: www.conceptpub.com

Cataloging in Publication--Courtesy: D.K. Agencies (P) Ltd. <docinfo@dkagencies.com>

Mohapatra, Ranjan Kumar, author.
Plain speak management : insights from life's lessons / Dr. Ranjan Kumar Mohapatra (Ph.D).
pages cm
ISBN 9789363445369 (HB)
ISBN 9789363446847 (PB)

1. Success. 2. Self-help techniques. 3. Conduct of life. I. Title.

LCC BF632.M64 2025 | DDC 158.1 23

Dedication

This book is dedicated to my parents.

To my Father, who spent first eighty years of his life dedicated to benefits of people; be as a part of his official engagement or social commitment or family obligation. He never cared for what will happen in future, as long as it serves the people around him, that day! As I see him now, he has become a small child, suffering from acute dementia, yet maintaining the same spirit. He does not recognise us so fluently, so easily, yet he treats us as human beings, with utmost respect and care. There have been bad days too, with his child-like temper running high. But the moment, that is over, he is back to being the loving and caring gentleman, that he is.

To my Mother, who has been an epitome of patience, perseverance, and affection. Though she got married at a tender age of thirteen, when she was just in class nine, she was the Guru to all we siblings. She was the first Maths teacher, first Hindi teacher, first English teacher to all of us. If I try to call myself a lifelong learner, it is my mother, who manifested it day in and day out. If she taught us anything, she took her turn to learn it herself, while discharging her roles and responsibilities of being the lifeline not only for us, but for a host of our relations. It was a big big family, she took care of and yet her appetite for learning never diminished. She published her first book of Odia poetry "Bhaba Arghya" at the age of seventy four!! And still, she is in the learning mode, writing poetry almost on a daily basis, while taking care of my father single-handedly.

I dedicate this book to these two wonderful human beings, who have been beacons of hope for me, all through out.

Thank you Nana and Bou for being there always for me and making me whatever I am today.

Foreword

This book contains the wisdom of a lifetime, presented to us in beautiful, byte-sized chapters which are a delight to read. Professionals of all hues can learn from these thoughts and reflections pertaining to so many situations that we are very likely to encounter during the course of our lives. In these pages, you will find stories and insights, but, most importantly, you will discover candid wisdom, born out of the author's desire to share his knowledge as frankly as possible.

I have known the author, Ranjan Kumar Mohapatra, for over forty years now. I first met him when both he and I were young undergraduate students at the Birla Institute of Technology and Science (BITS), Pilani. In the four years we spent together on college campus, his friendship and advice was a source of great support to me. His positive energy rubbed off on many of us at that time, as it does even today, through the pages of this wonderful book.

That is one of the key elements which makes this book special. It contains not just wisdom, but a constant stream of positive energy that nudges us to move in all the right directions, particularly when we are at a crossroads. Be it finding joy in the everyday moments of life or triumphing through faith and resilience, this book is all about finding the path that will move us towards higher planes of happiness and fulfilment. Ranjan's words sparkle with pragmatic wisdom and the desire to live the best life that we can, whatever be the circumstances that we are faced with.

Some of the topics that he deals with in this book are often areas of discomfort – such as managing partings with people or embracing impermanence. Other topics – such as acknowledging the unsung heroes who make our lives comfortable or the power of gratitude – touch on blind spots which we often miss out on. And yet other topics – such as finding meaning in adversity or transforming challenges into triumphs – are about dipping into the strength that exists deep within us, if only we know how and where to find it.

Across all these diverse areas, Ranjan has woven simple, powerful narratives based on his beliefs. In each chapter, he brings these convictions to life through real-life stories drawn from many worlds, including history, sports, literature, business, science and music. These stories not only make their points very well, but collectively they also represent a treasure trove of inspiration that can bring out the best in us.

Here is a book that you can dip into at leisure, and does not require sequential reading at all. Every chapter is self contained. Therefore, if you wish to, you could read the sections that appear most relevant to you at any point in time. However, taken in aggregate, this book becomes a very useful guidebook that can help you reflect deeply and develop your own plans of action.

Ranjan writes thoughtfully, and many of his insights in these pages have made me sit up and say – Why did I not think about this before? I would like to thank him for writing and compiling these essays, because they help illuminate our journeys. This book helps us shut out the noise and listen to the music.

Bangalore
25th November 2024

Harish Bhat
Former Brand Custodian, Tata Sons
Avid Marketer and bestselling author

Reflections

In Plain Speak Management, Ranjan Kumar Mohapatra offers a heartfelt exploration of leadership and personal growth, drawing from everyday experiences and extraordinary stories. From resilience and positivity to embracing impermanence, each chapter weaves practical wisdom with timeless values to inspire readers to navigate life's challenges and opportunities. Perfect for seasoned professionals and lifelong learners alike, this book encourages us to lead with authenticity, cherish meaningful relationships, and strive for collective success.

Johnny C. Taylor, Jr.,
SHRM-SCP,
President and Chief Executive Officer, SHRM

Plain Speak Management is simply conveying key life lessons like Resilience, Perseverance, Collaboration & Positivity through real life stories of inspiring personalities like Mandela & Edison among others. Ranjan Kumar Mohapatra's work is an essential tool kit on the "soft skills" essential to build a successful career or business . Essential reading for the young and refresher for the seasoned!

Suresh Narayanan
Chairman & MD,
Nestle India Ltd.

Ranjan Kumar Mohapatra has distilled his years of impressive experience in this fine book. Very easy to read, powerful triggers for reflection, each chapter makes so much sense. You could start from anywhere and traverse as your own questions demand. A must read for anyone who is feeling low or high. This is such a unique gift to all.

Prabir Jha
Founder & CEO,
Prabir Jha People Advisory

Plain Speak Management, epitomises the thoughts as well as practices Dr. Ranjan Kumar Mohapatra has demonstrated during his long stint as a Corporate Management Practitioner. The book reinforces these thoughts with real life examples from the world, we see around us, be it philanthropy, or sports or innovations or literature. The connect the book creates with the readers is phenomenal. The positivity in life is re-emphasized from time to time and this can work as morale boosters for readers from all ages!

Dr. Amit Bhalla
Vice President,
Manav Rachna Educational Institution

Plain Speak Management is an authentically inspiring and thought-provoking book that blends personal reflections, historical anecdotes, and timeless life lessons. Rooted in the author's experiences, it offers invaluable insights on resilience, adaptability, and the power of human connections. Drawing from stories of legendary real life historical figures, the book demonstrates the universal applicability of perseverance, collaboration, and ethical leadership. Through engaging stories and practical wisdom, it encourages readers to embrace life's uncertainties with an open mind and a learning spirit. Ultimately, Plain Speak Management is a heartfelt guide to personal and professional growth. Congratulations to Dr. Ranjan Kumar Mohapatra for this labour of love.

Ms. Anuradha Razdan
CHRO-Beauty & Wellbeing and Global Equity,
Diversity & Inclusion Officer, Unilever Plc

Plain Speak Management offers an ultimate refreshing blend of management wisdom and personal reflection. Drawing inspiration from diverse sources, including history, mythology, and personal experiences, the book delves into universal themes like perseverance, adaptability, and ethical leadership. The author's engaging writing style and relatable anecdotes make the book accessible to a wide audience. Whether you're a seasoned professional or a budding leader, this book provides valuable insights that can be applied to both personal and professional life. It's a captivating read that inspires readers to embrace challenges, seek growth, and make a positive impact.

Mr. G. Krishnakumar
Chairman & Managing Director,
Bharat Petroleum Corporation Ltd.

Prologue

The year 2023 saw a lot of roller coaster ride for me professionally. Sometimes, it was too hot, some other time, it was chilly for me. And then in the month of May, the change happened. Probably, I was looking for such an event, which would provide me an opportunity to live my dreams.

That is when I decided to start posting my ***PSTO (Plain Speak – Thoughts Only)*** in the social media on a daily basis. The first posting came on June 1st, 2023.

Incidentally, when I was posted in Mauritius, I used to write a weekly column in the sole English Newspaper there. I had christened it as ***Plain Speak Only***. So, when I decided to post the daily thoughts, I just extended the same to ***'Thoughts' only***.

Life is a great learning experience. When we go through it, there comes those pearls of learning, continuously and from all quarters. So, my efforts have been to just put it across. When I started it, I was not sure, if I would be able to continue. But I received supports, appreciation from many unexpected quarters. Many built on it. Many gave counter opinions. Many just liked it and moved on. But all these certainly gave me the energy, which I probably needed, to continue posting it daily.

In one of such occasions, a young colleague of mine Ms Anantika Nandy from our Haldia Refinery wrote me these encouraging words:

Quote

Dear Sir,

A fellow IOCian from Haldia, I follow your thoughts on this platform. Your point of views have great depth; personally speaking they help me pull myself out of tough times and ask the proper question suitable for the situation, and not whine.

It's a humble request coming from a very very junior person like me, but you could convert your thoughts into a book & publish them.

I think everyone will benefit from that.

Thank you Sir.

Regards.

Anantika Nandy, Haldia

Unquote

Exactly like what would have happened to anyone else, I was simply touched. This, definitely, planted the seeds in my mind to convert these thoughts into a book.

The question then came as to how do I go ahead.

Our society, our world is full of examples of great persons, who have probably lived these thoughts. Yet, many of us do not know the details. I felt, could I bring in reference to these personalities, living, or dead or organisations or occurrences and, and thus encourage readers to make efforts to know more about them?

And that became the starting point of this book.

In this book, I have tried to expand my thoughts with the live experience of people, or Organisations or events all around the world. Many of them are known, but quite a few are also those unknown warriors, influencers or leaders, who have lived the essence of life and have made a positive difference to the world.

Each chapter is based on the thoughts, I posted, numbered as ***PSTO-1*** onwards and I have tried to link that to the personalities, who resonated with the thought. I have a vision that this will definitely encourage readers to explore more about these personalities. Some of the personalities, in this book, may have appeared on multiple occasions. You may view it as a bit of my bias or the magnitude of their work and contribution to the world! At the same time, there is a caveat. These are not the only personalities who displayed these qualities, for each example, there are thousand other, whom I have not covered.

I hope the readers too find resonance with the thoughts based on their own experiences as well.

Happy reading.

Acknowledgements

Going through the process of assimilating your thoughts, though quite enjoyable, is a tedious process too. But as they say, people around you, sometimes from unexpected quarters, do come forward to extend their helping hands ensure that your dream gets realised. Acknowledging their role and contribution is quite a small tribute from my side.

I have dedicated my maiden effort to my parents and without their support and their blessings, this book would never have been possible.

Nibedita, my wife, has been a consistent supporter in this endeavour, as she does always for every move that I make. She, being a short story writer herself, has been highly advantageous to me. She gave me the space as well as constant encouragement to complete this book. Of course, the support was there also during the posting of my PSTOs. After 100th one, when I was seriously thinking of taking a break, her simply suggestion; "Why don't you complete 200 in this stretch?" probably boosted my energy and I could do it. I can't thank her enough for allowing me to work on multiple areas at the same time and never letting me worry about anything that I required to sustain.

I am truly indebted to my children, Nayan, Raman & Neha for being my mirror for bouncing back my thoughts and have a reality check from time to time. Nayan, the elder son, went through the entire draft meticulously and suggested many notable achievers and their feats, which I have included in the book. The fact that readers will find some star players and athletes in the book, is all courtesy Nayan, he being a sports enthusiast himself. Raman, the younger son, has been the technical guide to me in all respect. Thanks to him and his impeccable technical knowhow, compiling this book has been probably a bit easier. Neha, my daughter-in-law, herself an expert in language & expression, did the proof-reading with due care and professionalism. I am thankful to my children for being there always and standing behind me with a rock-soild support.

There are many people in my life, who have always encouraged me to write a book.

Today, when I venture to come out with my maiden book, I would like to acknowledge their encouragement. I humble remember my eldest cousin brother Mansij, Munu Bhaina, to me, who left us for heavenly abode too early, more than a decade back. He was the one, who would remind me every now & then, right after my class X, particularly during those Puja Celebrations at our ancestral place, Ranpur, that I must write books. I had promised to him, "Yes, I would" but had not given a timeline. Now that I am publishing my first book, I am missing him dearly and imagining how his face would have lit up seeing the book. "Miss you Munu Bhaina!!"

Two of my friends Bichitra Behura & Harish Bhat, themselves prolific poet and writer respectively, having brought out more than several books themselves, have always been pestering me to go for writing. It is their nudge, which, to an extent, pushed me into penning it. Thank you Harish & Bichitra.

Additionally, my heartfelt gratitude to Harish for agreeing to write the Foreword, despite his busy routine. Amidst his own heavy schedule of writing & speaking engagements, he could take out time to go through the entire manuscript and write the foreword, is a big testament of his commitment and love for creativity. Thank you Harish!

I am extremely thankful to Prof Dr. Vinaysheel Gautam, Founding Director of IIM, Khozikode and a Management Guru-par-excellence for encouraging me to make it happen. In his own unique style, he would cajole, sometimes admonish and many a times motivate me to go for it. Thank you Sir for instilling that confidence in me, which has culminated in the form of this book and hope many more to come, as you always emphasize.

I am extremely thankful to many of my friends, colleagues and professional acquaintances, who played a big role in my changed approach to life and probably helped a lot in making this book a reality. It would be really difficult to name all, I may need an exclusive book for that!! However, let me not leave the opportunity of express my since thanks to a few, who do represent this strong group. Thank you Mr. Makrand Nene, my guide, my conscience keeper in Indian Oil and always thereafter; Nehaa Choudhury, Anurag Shukla, Late Anirban Dasgupta, Vandana Singh, Deepali Pandey, Sheetal, Dr. Sandeep Sharma, some of my young and not-so-young brigade in Indian Oil, who not only went out of way and stood with me without fear or favour; some senior corporate leaders like Ayush Gupta, P. Dwarakanath, Dr. Alka Mittal, Dr. G. P. Rao, Rajesh Singh, Shridhar Bhagwat, Sukrit Dutta, Tanmoy Chatterjee, Anirban Ghosh and many others who stood by me and helped me certainly concentrate on my effort to find my footing. Special reverence and gratitude to Sri Anish Jee, who brought in a sense of calmness during those turbulent times and helped me concentrate on the present rather than worrying about future.

I am missing many, I know and I am extremely sorry for that. More about it when I come up with another effort specially on that.

I would like to thank my immediate family; my sisters and the families, my in-laws, my uncles and aunties, my cousins, my nephews and nieces, who somehow persisted with me for doing it, some way or the other. I am thankful to each one of them for their confidence.

Let me express my special thanks to Concept Publishing Company Pvt. Ltd., New Delhi for giving me this opportunity by publishing this maiden effort and providing all assistance.

Contents

1

Embracing Life's Surprises

The Power of Perseverance

PSTO-1: Life has its own way of surprising you. It's prudent therefore to never give up.

Life has a knack for throwing unexpected challenges our way, often when we least expect them. Just when we think we have it all figured out, a curveball comes hurtling toward us, leaving us to wonder how we'll ever navigate the uncertain terrain ahead. In these moments, it's easy to feel defeated, to consider giving up. But it is precisely during these times that we should remember; "Life has its own way of surprising you. It's prudent therefore to never give up."

Let me delve into this by exploring some live examples of individuals who faced adversity head-on and emerged stronger and wiser.

1. Thomas Edison and the Light Bulb

Thomas Edison, one of history's greatest inventors, encountered countless failures on his journey to create the incandescent light bulb. He once famously said, "I have not failed. I've just found

10,000 ways that won't work." Edison's relentless determination ultimately led to the successful invention of the light bulb, which forever changed the world. His story teaches us that setbacks are often steppingstones to success if we refuse to give up.

2. J.K. Rowling and the Harry Potter Series

Before becoming a household name, J.K. Rowling faced rejection after rejection from publishers for her Harry Potter manuscript. She was a struggling single mother at that time, and her life was far from easy. However, she persevered, believing in her story and her dream. Today, the Harry Potter series has sold over 500 million copies worldwide, demonstrating the extraordinary possibilities that can arise when we persist in the face of adversity.

3. The Wright Brothers and the First Powered Flight

Orville and Wilbur Wright's dream of human flight seemed absurd to many in their time. They faced numerous failures and setbacks as they designed and tested their flying machines. On December 17, 1903, in Kitty Hawk, North Carolina, the Wright brothers achieved their dream with the world's first powered, controlled, and sustained flight. Their unwavering commitment to their vision changed the course of history.

4. Nelson Mandela's Fight for Equality

Nelson Mandela's life was marked by adversity and injustice. He spent 27 years in prison for his opposition to apartheid in South Africa. However, he emerged from prison with a commitment to reconciliation and equality. Mandela's perseverance and steadfast belief in a better future led to the dismantling of apartheid and his election as South Africa's first black president.

These examples underscore the importance of resilience and the refusal to surrender in the face of life's surprises. Life is full of challenges, but it is also brimming with opportunities for growth, learning, and transformation. When we encounter setbacks and difficulties, it's essential to view them as steppingstones, not stumbling blocks.

In conclusion, life's surprises may be daunting, but they also hold the potential for incredible personal growth and achievement. The stories of Edison, Rowling, the Wright brothers, and Mandela remind us that the path to success is rarely linear, but those who persevere, even in the face of adversity, can achieve greatness. So, we must embrace life's surprises with open hearts, knowing that by never giving up, we can shape our destinies and create a brighter future for ourselves and others.

2

The Contagious Power of Smiles

A Lesson from Hindu Mythology

PSTO-2: Smiling is one of the most preferred contagious 'disorders'. Spread it.

In a world often filled with challenges and uncertainties, a simple act of kindness can have a profound impact on someone's day. Among these acts, to me smiling stands out as one of the most preferred and contagious "disorders" one can spread. This universal gesture transcends language barriers, cultural divides, and even time itself, as evidenced by timeless stories from Hindu mythology that showcase the enduring power of a smile.

1. The Divine Smile of Lord Krishna

In Hinduism, Lord Krishna is often depicted with a charming and mischievous smile, which has endeared him to millions. One of the most famous stories associated with Krishna's smile is the tale of the "Ras Leela," where he dances with the Gopis (milkmaids) of Vrindavan. It is said that Krishna's enchanting smile during this divine dance filled the hearts of the Gopis with unparalleled joy and happiness.

Krishna's smile is a reminder that a genuine smile can not only bring joy to others but also create an atmosphere of love and unity. Just like Krishna's smile, a warm and heartfelt smile has the power to lift spirits and foster a sense of togetherness.

2. The Smile of Lord Ganesha

Lord Ganesha, the elephant-headed god of wisdom and prosperity, is another prominent figure in Hindu mythology. His childlike smile represents innocence and purity of heart. According to one popular legend, Ganesha's smile played a pivotal role in teaching invaluable lessons about humility and the art of spreading joy.

In this story, Ganesha competes in a race with his brother Kartikeya. Ganesha, with his stubby elephant legs, couldn't match Kartikeya's speed. However, Ganesha circumambulated his parents, Lord Shiva and Goddess Parvati, with devotion, signifying that they were his world. His parents were deeply moved by this gesture, and their smiles illuminated the heavens.

This tale teaches us that a humble and genuine smile can win hearts and create moments of profound connection. Ganesha's smile exemplifies the idea that joy can be found in the simple act of embracing one's true self and appreciating the love that surrounds us.

3. The Smile of Hanuman

Hanuman, the devoted disciple of Lord Rama, is renowned for his unwavering loyalty and boundless love. His smile reflects his devotion and selflessness. One of the most touching moments in the *Ramayana* is when Hanuman, while searching for a medicinal herb, inadvertently lifts an entire mountain to save Lakshmana's life.

Hanuman's smile, as he holds the mountain aloft, is a symbol of the extraordinary strength that lies within us when we act out of love and selflessness. His story tells us that a smile born from selfless service and dedication can move mountains and inspire others to do the same.

In conclusion, smiles have unrestricted power. Hindu mythology offers profound insights into the contagious power of smiles. The smiles of Lord Krishna, Lord Ganesha, and Hanuman not only bring joy and happiness but also convey timeless lessons about love, humility, and selflessness. In our own lives, we can feel that a simple smile has the potential to brighten someone's day, foster unity, and spread positivity. So, we must make this "contagious disorder" of smiling a part of our life and share its warmth with the world, just as these divine beings did in the sacred stories of Hindu mythology.

3

The Significance of Looking Down Before Looking Up

Lessons from Science and Beyond

PSTO-3: Looking up is very important, but a look down before you look up is much more important, much more desirable.

In our quest for progress and innovation, the act of looking up and aspiring to new heights is often celebrated. We admire visionaries who set their sights on the stars and dream big. However, there's an essential precursor to this upward gaze: looking down. The process of introspection, understanding, and laying strong foundations is equally, if not more, crucial. We have scores of examples from the world of science, technology, to underscore this.

1. Isaac Newton and the Falling Apple

One of the most iconic moments in the history of science is Sir Isaac Newton's realization of gravity. Legend has it that Newton, while sitting under an apple tree, observed an apple falling to the ground. Instead of merely marvelling at the sight, he asked why the apple fell down. This simple act of looking down, both literally and metaphorically, led to his groundbreaking theory of gravity. Newton's introspection and curiosity paved the way for the laws of motion and modern physics.

2. Silicon Valley's Success Stories

In the world of technology and entrepreneurship, Silicon Valley is renowned for its innovative spirit. While we often hear about the companies that have reached the pinnacle of success, what's equally important is the culture of self-reflection and learning from failure. Many successful tech leaders, including Steve Jobs, have emphasized the significance of looking down to understand past mistakes and challenges before embarking on new ventures. Apple, for instance, experienced setbacks in the 1990s, but its introspective approach and focus on user-centric design led to its resurgence.

3. Medical Breakthroughs

In the field of medicine, looking down through rigorous research and diagnostic processes is fundamental to making advancements. For example, the discovery of antibiotics by Alexander Fleming came about because he took the time to investigate why some bacterial cultures in his laboratory were not growing as expected. His keen observation of a "contaminated" culture plate paved the way for the development of penicillin and revolutionized modern medicine.

4. Environmental Conservation

When it comes to addressing environmental challenges, looking down is indispensable, once again both literally and metaphorically. Conservationists and environmentalists recognize the importance of studying ecosystems, tracking biodiversity, and understanding the impact of human activity on the planet. This introspective approach is essential for devising sustainable solutions to protect our environment for future generations.

In conclusion, the act of looking up and aiming high is undoubtedly crucial for innovation and progress. However, it is equally vital to remember that looking down—engaging in introspection, understanding our foundations, and learning from our past—is the cornerstone of sustainable growth and success. Just as great scientists, innovators, and leaders have demonstrated, a balanced approach that combines ambition with self-awareness can lead to enduring achievements and positive change, both in the world of science and in our personal lives.

4

Embracing Impermanence

The Path to a Fulfilling Life

PSTO-4: Nothing is permanent in life. Sooner we realise it, better our life becomes.

Life is an ever-changing journey, a continuous ebb and flow of experiences, emotions, and circumstances. In this dynamic existence, one universal truth stands clear: nothing is permanent. The sooner we grasp the essence of impermanence, the better equipped we become to navigate life's twists and turns. In this chapter, an attempt is made to explore this wisdom with live examples that illustrate the transformative power of accepting impermanence.

1. The Changing Seasons

Nature provides us with a vivid example of impermanence through the changing seasons. Winter turns to spring, spring to summer, and so on. Each season brings its unique beauty and challenges. People who embrace the impermanence of seasons adapt, finding joy in the first snowfall and blooming flowers, while also appreciating the warmth of summer and the colors of autumn. Just as nature evolves, so do our lives, and understanding this cyclical nature can bring a sense of harmony and acceptance.

2. The Ever-Transforming Career Landscape

In the realm of work and career, impermanence is particularly evident. The job market evolves, industries rise and fall, and technological advancements reshape professions. Those who acknowledge the transient nature of their careers remain open to growth and change. For example, consider individuals who once worked in traditional roles but adapted to the digital age, thriving in new domains as technology evolved.

3. Relationships and Friendships

Human relationships, too, are subject to impermanence. Friends and loved ones may come and go, whether through changing life circumstances or the passage of time. People who grasp the impermanence of relationships cherish the moments spent with loved ones, knowing that each interaction is a gift. They appreciate the lessons learned from connections, even when those connections evolve or fade.

4. Impermanence in Success

Success creates a halo around the leaders that it is permanent. History is filled with examples of then considered invincible leaders succumbing swiftly to their own downfalls. The rise and fall of Julius Caesar is a timeless example of the impermanence of power. He went from being a Roman general at the height of his influence to meeting his tragic end at the hands of a conspiracy. Caesar's life illustrates that even the most dominant individuals are not immune to the impermanence of life's fortunes.

5. Achievements beyond Personal Setbacks

Everyone faces setbacks or impedances during one's lives. But people, who realise that these are short-term and never permanent, they rise above those and succeed in life. Vincent van Gogh is now celebrated as one of the greatest painters in history. But during his lifetime, he struggled in obscurity and battled mental health issues. His story reminds us that the value and recognition of one's accomplishments can change dramatically over time. Impermanence affects how the world perceives and appreciates our achievements.

By embracing the impermanence of life, we open ourselves to a profound sense of freedom. We release the anxiety and resistance that often accompany change and uncertainty. Instead, we find the courage to pursue our passions, take risks, and savour each moment. Impermanence invites us to live in the present, to appreciate what we have, and to let go of what no longer serves us.

In conclusion, the realization that nothing is permanent in life is a powerful catalyst for personal growth and fulfilment. It enables us to flow with life's currents, adapting and evolving as needed. By learning from the changing seasons, career shifts, evolving relationships, health challenges, and the practice of mindfulness, we can lead richer, more meaningful lives. Embracing impermanence isn't a sign of vulnerability; it's a testament to our resilience and capacity to find joy and wisdom in the ever-changing tapestry of existence.

5

The Triumph of Togetherness

Winning the Race Together

PSTO-5: Winning the race is important, but winning the race together is fabulous.

In a world often fixated on individual achievements and personal victories, there exists a profound truth: winning the race together is nothing short of fabulous. While individual accomplishments are noteworthy, the magic truly happens when people unite their efforts, supporting and uplifting each other to reach a common goal. In this chapter, an effort is made to explore this concept through examples from the world of sports and beyond, where teamwork and collaboration reign supreme.

1. Relay Races in Athletics

In the world of sports, relay races stand as a testament to the beauty of winning together. Take, for instance, the 4x100 meters relay in athletics. In this event, four sprinters come together, each running their segment of the race. Success hinges not only on the speed of each individual but also on the seamless baton handoffs and the collective effort of the team. The exhilaration of crossing the finish line as one, victorious and united, transcends individual accolades.

2. The Miracle on Ice - 1980 U.S. Olympic Hockey Team

One of the most iconic moments in sports history came during the 1980 Winter Olympics when the U.S. Olympic ice hockey team, composed of young amateur players, defeated the seemingly invincible Soviet Union team. The victory was not merely about winning a game; it was a triumph of teamwork, determination, and the belief that together, they could achieve the impossible. The players' camaraderie and unity made their victory resonate far beyond the ice rink.

3. SpaceX's Historic Crewed Launch

In the realm of space exploration, SpaceX's historic crewed launch in 2020 demonstrated the power of collaboration in the face of the unknown. Astronauts Doug Hurley and Bob Behnken embarked on the first crewed mission by a private company, SpaceX, to the International Space Station. Their journey symbolized the incredible achievements possible when public and private sectors work together, pooling their expertise and resources to achieve a common goal.

4. Collaborative Scientific Discoveries

Scientific breakthroughs often result from the collaborative efforts of researchers from various disciplines. For instance, the discovery of the Higgs boson particle at CERN's Large Hadron Collider required the collaboration of thousands of scientists and engineers from around the world. Their combined expertise and dedication paved the way for a profound advancement in our understanding of the universe.

5. Community Initiatives and Volunteering

Beyond the realm of sports and science, community initiatives and volunteering highlight the extraordinary impact of winning together. When individuals come together to address pressing social issues, such as poverty, environmental conservation, or disaster relief, their collective efforts create lasting change. These initiatives demonstrate that when people unite for a common cause, the victories extend far beyond personal gain.

In conclusion, the notion of winning the race together encapsulates the essence of human achievement at its finest. Whether on the sports field, in the exploration of space, in scientific endeavours, or through community initiatives, the beauty of collaboration lies in the shared joy of success and the lasting bonds forged in pursuit of a common goal. It reminds us that while individual accomplishments have their place, the most fabulous victories are those achieved together, where the sum is greater than its parts, and the journey itself becomes a celebration of unity and shared purpose.

6

Embracing the Infinite Quest for Knowledge

Making Every Moment Count

PSTO-6: There are so many things to learn. I wonder if one life is enough. It is incumbent on us to make every moment count.

In a world teeming with knowledge, where the universe's mysteries, art's nuances, and science's intricacies beckon, it's only natural to wonder if a single lifetime is enough to satiate our thirst for learning. Yet, it is precisely this insatiable curiosity and the recognition of life's fleeting nature that propel us to make every moment count. Let's embark on a journey that celebrates the pursuit of knowledge and its profound impact on our lives, drawing inspiration from the world of literature and beyond.

1. The Endless World of Literature

Literature, a vast realm of stories, ideas, and emotions, exemplifies the boundless nature of knowledge. Consider the works of prolific authors like William Shakespeare, whose timeless plays and sonnets continue to captivate readers across centuries. Each of Shakespeare's creations offers a window into the human condition, reminding us that a lifetime's exploration may only scratch the surface of literary treasures.

2. The Voyager Space Probes

In the realm of science and exploration, the Voyager 1 and 2 space probes provide a poignant example. Launched in 1977 to explore the outer planets, these probes now venture beyond our solar system, carrying a message from Earth in the form of the Golden Record. The record contains sounds and images representing our diverse planet. Though the probes themselves will continue their journey long after our lifetimes, they remind us of humanity's relentless quest for knowledge and the timeless echo of our existence.

3. The Renaissance Minds of Leonardo da Vinci

The polymath Leonardo da Vinci serves as an embodiment of a lifetime dedication to learning. His insatiable curiosity led him to explore fields as diverse as art, anatomy, engineering, and mathematics. Leonardo's notebooks, filled with sketches and observations, are a testament to a life committed to making every moment count through the pursuit of knowledge. His legacy continues to inspire generations.

4. Continuous Self-Improvement

In our personal lives, the pursuit of knowledge is not limited to academia or formal education. It extends to self-improvement and personal growth. Individuals who strive to learn, adapt, and evolve in various aspects of their lives demonstrate the beauty of making every moment count. Whether through developing new skills, exploring new hobbies, or fostering meaningful relationships, these pursuits enrich their existence.

5. The Quest for a Sustainable Future

The pursuit of knowledge is also evident in humanity's efforts to address global challenges. Scientists, activists, and innovators worldwide dedicate their lives to understanding and combating issues like climate change, poverty, and disease. Their collective knowledge and relentless determination underscore the imperative to make every moment count for the betterment of our planet and its inhabitants.

In conclusion, the recognition that a single lifetime may not be sufficient to grasp the entirety of human knowledge is both humbling and invigorating. It invites us to embark on an infinite quest for understanding, to explore the uncharted territories of science, art, and self-discovery. Every moment presents an opportunity to learn, grow, and contribute to the collective tapestry of human knowledge. It reminds us that, despite the vastness of the universe, our ability to make each moment count is a testament to the resilience of the human spirit and the enduring quest for enlightenment.

7

Finding Joy in the Everyday Moments

A Reminder to Embrace Happiness

PSTO-7: Whenever you feel sad, just look around. You will get so many reasons to be happy again.

Life, with its ebbs and flows, often brings moments of sadness and despair. During these times, it's easy to become consumed by our troubles, losing sight of the beauty that surrounds us. Yet, a simple shift in perspective can reveal a profound truth: even in the darkest moments, there are countless reasons to be happy. Let's explore this uplifting concept with live examples that demonstrate the power of finding happiness in everyday life.

1. The Beauty of Nature

Nature, with its awe-inspiring landscapes and intricate ecosystems, offers a wellspring of reasons to be happy. Take a moment to look around and marvel at the vibrant colors of a blooming flower, the soothing sound of a babbling brook, or the gentle rustling of leaves in a forest. Nature's beauty is a constant reminder that happiness can be found in the simplest of things.

2. Acts of Kindness

Even in the face of personal sorrow, acts of kindness from others can lift our spirits. Consider the example of a stranger who holds the door for you or a friend who offers a comforting word or a warm embrace when you're feeling down. These small but meaningful gestures remind us that human connection and compassion are sources of profound happiness.

3. The Joy of Learning

The pursuit of knowledge is an endless source of happiness. Whether it's discovering a fascinating fact, learning a new skill, or diving into a captivating book, the act of learning opens doors to joy and fulfilment. The world is a vast classroom, and every moment presents an opportunity to expand our understanding.

4. The Innocence of Children

The laughter and innocence of children have a unique ability to uplift our spirits. A child's smile, a playful giggle, or their unfiltered curiosity can dispel sadness in an instant. Their presence serves as a reminder that happiness often resides in the simplicity of the present moment.

5. Moments of Serenity

In the hustle and bustle of daily life, we often overlook moments of serenity. Whether it's the tranquillity of a quiet morning, the peacefulness of a starry night, or the stillness of a meditation session, these moments offer solace and reasons to be happy. They remind us that happiness can be found in the pause between life's demands.

In conclusion, the notion that we can find reasons to be happy even in times of sadness is a testament to the resilience of the human spirit. Life is a tapestry of experiences, and each thread, whether light or dark, contributes to our growth and understanding. By taking a moment to look around and appreciate the beauty, kindness, learning, innocence, serenity, and personal achievements that surround us, we can rediscover happiness even in the midst of sorrow. These moments of joy, like beacons of light, guide us through the challenges of life, reminding us that happiness is always within reach, waiting to be embraced.

8

The Path to Success

Bringing Smiles to Co-travellers

PSTO-8: There are several ways, one can reach the Goal. But the path, which would bring in smiles in the faces of the co-travellers, must be the preferred one.

Life is a journey, and each of us has goals and aspirations we aim to achieve. Along the way, we encounter numerous paths, each offering its own set of challenges and opportunities. Yet, there is a profound wisdom in choosing the path that not only leads to our own success but also brings smiles to the faces of those who accompany us on this journey. The universe is full of many instances, which are worth recapitulating.

1. Leadership in Business

In the corporate world, leaders who prioritize the happiness and well-being of their teams often achieve remarkable success. Take the example of Tony Hsieh, the former CEO of Zappos. He fostered a workplace culture centred on employee satisfaction and happiness. His leadership philosophy was simple: "If you get the culture right, most of the other stuff will just take care of itself." By prioritizing the happiness of his co-workers, Zappos became renowned not only for its exceptional customer service but also as a great place to work.

2. Education and Mentorship

In education and mentorship, educators who are dedicated to not just imparting knowledge but also nurturing the growth and happiness of their students have a lasting impact. Educators like Jaime Escalante, portrayed in the movie "Stand and Deliver," transformed the lives of disadvantaged students by believing in their potential and helping them achieve academic success. His commitment to his students brought smiles to their faces as they achieved academic excellence against all odds.

3. Philanthropy and Giving Back

Philanthropists who choose paths of giving and social responsibility not only achieve personal fulfilment but also bring smiles to countless beneficiaries. Bill and Melinda Gates, through their foundation, have devoted their wealth and resources to improving global health and reducing poverty. Their efforts have saved lives, empowered communities, and inspired others to join the cause of philanthropy, spreading smiles to those in need.

4. Personal Relationships

In our personal lives, the paths we choose in our relationships have a profound impact on the happiness of our loved ones. Couples who prioritize communication, empathy, and compromise often build stronger and more fulfilling partnerships. Such relationships not only bring smiles to each other's faces but also create an environment of love and harmony that extends to their families and friends.

In conclusion, the journey toward our goals is not a solitary one. Along the way, we travel with co-passengers, whether they be colleagues, fellow activists, students, beneficiaries, or loved ones. Choosing a path that brings smiles to their faces is not only a testament to our humanity but also a recipe for enduring success and fulfilment. The examples of leaders, environmentalists, educators, philanthropists, and those in personal relationships underscore the transformative power of prioritizing the happiness and well-being of co-travellers on the path to success. In doing so, we not only achieve our goals but also leave a positive and lasting impact on the world around us.

9

Leading with Resilience

Celebrating Failures as Catalysts for Growth

PSTO-9: As a leader, we must learn to celebrate failures. At the end of the day, these learnings from the so-called failures, make the team strong and resolute.

In the realm of leadership, there exists a profound wisdom: the ability to celebrate failures. While success is often the goal, it is through setbacks and so-called failures that leaders and their teams learn, adapt, and ultimately become stronger and more resilient. In this chapter, let us explore the significance of embracing failure as a valuable learning tool, supported by some real-world examples from various fields.

1. The Silicon Valley Mindset

In the dynamic and competitive world of technology and innovation, Silicon Valley stands as a testament to the culture of celebrating failures. Startups and tech giants alike understand that each setback represents a valuable learning opportunity. For instance, the story of Airbnb's early struggles is a classic example.

The founders faced rejection from investors and encountered numerous challenges. However, their resilience and commitment to learning from failures eventually led to the creation of a global hospitality giant.

2. NASA's Mars Exploration Program

In the field of space exploration, NASA's Mars missions provide compelling illustrations of embracing failures. The Mars program has seen its share of setbacks, with numerous missions ending in failure. However, these challenges have not deterred NASA but have instead propelled the organization to improve and adapt. The famous phrase "Failure is not an option" encapsulates NASA's commitment to learning from mistakes and continuously refining their approach to exploration.

3. Sports Leadership

Sports, with its emphasis on teamwork and resilience, offers valuable leadership lessons. Coaches often play a pivotal role in fostering a culture where failures are seen as opportunities for growth. Consider the example of Phil Jackson, the legendary coach of the Chicago Bulls and the Los Angeles Lakers. He understood the importance of celebrating losses as chances to improve. His teams learned from defeats, adjusted their strategies, and came back stronger, achieving multiple championships.

4. Medical Research and Drug Development

In the realm of medical research and drug development, failures are an inherent part of the process. Many groundbreaking medical discoveries have arisen from experiments that initially yielded unexpected results or setbacks. The discovery of penicillin by Alexander Fleming, already we have seen in the earlier chapter, emerged from a petri dish that had become contaminated. Fleming's openness to learning from this apparent failure led to the development of one of the most crucial antibiotics in medical history.

In conclusion, celebrating failures as a leader is a testament to resilience and a commitment to growth. Whether in the tech industry, space exploration, sports, medical research, or personal life, the ability to turn setbacks into learning is a hallmark of effective leadership. By creating an environment where failures are viewed as opportunities for learning and improvement, leaders empower their teams to become stronger, more innovative, and more resilient. The examples from various fields underscore the transformative power of embracing failure as a catalyst for growth, ultimately leading to greater success and achievement.

10

Embracing the Power of Control

Capitalizing on the Controllable

PSTO-10: If we look at our lives, we realize we are in control of more than ninety percent of the events. Yet we tend to bother much more for the balance that are not under our control. As a result, we forget to capitalise on the controllable ones.

In the intricate tapestry of life, we often find ourselves grappling with the tug of events beyond our control, all the while overlooking the vast territory of decisions and actions firmly within our grasp. It's a human tendency to fret over the balance that eludes our influence, but what if we shifted our focus to harness the potential of the controllable? We must move forward by recognizing and capitalizing on the aspects we can control. We can navigate life's challenges with greater wisdom and fulfilment, supported by examples from various domains.

1. Health and Well-being

One of the most prominent areas where we exercise control is our health and well-being. Our daily choices regarding nutrition, exercise, sleep, and stress management significantly impact our physical and mental health. For instance, individuals who prioritize a balanced diet and regular exercise are more likely to enjoy improved health outcomes and a higher quality of life. By taking control of these factors, they capitalize on the controllable aspects of their well-being.

2. Financial Management

Financial security is another arena where our decisions play a pivotal role. Saving, investing, and budgeting are all controllable actions that can shape our financial future. A prudent investor who makes informed decisions and adheres to a disciplined financial plan is more likely to achieve long-term financial success.

3. Education and Personal Growth

Our quest for knowledge and personal growth is a realm where we wield significant control. The choice to pursue education, acquire new skills, or engage in continuous learning is entirely within our power. Examples abound of individuals who leveraged their passion for self-improvement to achieve remarkable success in their chosen fields.

4. Relationships and Communication

The quality of our relationships and communication is greatly influenced by our actions and choices. Effective communication, active listening, and empathy are controllable behaviors that contribute to healthy and fulfilling relationships. Those who invest in mastering these skills often enjoy more harmonious personal and professional connections.

5. Time Management and Productivity

Time, our most precious resource, is subject to our control. Effective time management and productivity practices can significantly impact our achievements and well-being. Leaders who prioritize tasks, set goals, and maintain focus capitalize on the controllable aspect of their daily routines.

6. Career Advancement

Advancing in one's career involves a combination of skills, networking, and effort—all of which are within our control. Individuals who invest in professional development, seek out mentorship, and take initiative often find themselves well-positioned for career growth.

In conclusion, the realization that we are in control of a significant portion of our lives can be empowering. By focusing our energy and attention on the controllable aspects, we can channel our efforts toward positive change and personal growth. Real-life examples from health, finance, education, relationships, time management, and career advancement illustrate the transformative power of recognizing and capitalizing on what is within our grasp. While it's natural to acknowledge the existence of external factors beyond our control, it is our choices and actions in the face of these circumstances that define our journey and ultimately lead to a life of fulfilment and success.

11

The Radiance of Positivity

Illuminating Your World and Beyond

PSTO-11: Stay positive on all occasions. It not only boosts you up, it also lights up the entire ecosystem surrounding you.

In the grand symphony of life, the role of positivity is akin to a radiant sun, casting its warm and uplifting light upon everything it touches. Embracing a positive mindset not only elevates our own spirits but also has the remarkable ability to illuminate the entire ecosystem that surrounds us. We can appreciate the transformative power of positivity and its far-reaching effects, supported by real-life examples from various aspects of life.

1. Overcoming Adversity with Positivity

Consider the remarkable story of Malala Yousafzai, the Pakistani activist and Nobel laureate. Malala's life took a dramatic turn when, at the age of 15, she was shot by the Taliban for advocating girls' education in Pakistan. Despite this life-threatening adversity, Malala remained incredibly positive and unwavering in her commitment to education.

During her recovery, Malala's positivity shone brightly. She used her ordeal as a platform to advocate even more passionately for girls' education worldwide. Her unyielding optimism and determination not only aided her own healing process but also inspired countless others to join her cause. Malala's story reminds us that even in the face of the most daunting challenges, a positive mindset can be a beacon of hope and a catalyst for profound change.

2. Inspirational Leadership

In leadership, a positive attitude can inspire and mobilize teams to achieve remarkable outcomes. Leaders who radiate positivity not only boost team morale but also foster an environment of trust and collaboration. A contemporary example is Oprah Winfrey, whose optimism and ability to empower others have made her a respected leader and influential figure in media and philanthropy.

3. Acts of Empathy

Positivity often manifests in acts of empathy. When individuals choose to spread positivity through small acts of empathy or kindness, they create a ripple effect that touches countless lives. Consider the "Pay It Forward" movement, where individuals perform acts of empathy for strangers with the simple request that the recipients do the same for others. This chain of positivity has the power to transform communities and foster a sense of interconnectedness.

4. Health and Well-being

Maintaining a positive mindset is closely linked to improved health and well-being. Research suggests that optimism can lead to better physical and mental health outcomes. Individuals who approach life with a positive outlook tend to experience lower stress levels, stronger immune systems, and a greater sense of overall well-being. Let us take the example of Paulo Coelho, the celebrated writer. In his childhood, he was put to mental health institution, from where he attempted to escape. He was put to studying Law, from where he also escaped to become a hippie. Yet, he never left his passion for writing. He overcame personal struggle to become a write par excellence.

5. Social Change and Impact

Positivity can be a driving force for social change and impact. Activists and advocates who approach societal issues with optimism and a belief in positive change inspire others to join their causes. The civil rights movement led by figures like Martin Luther King Jr., who exuded unwavering positivity and hope, stands as a testament to the transformative power of optimism in driving societal change.

In conclusion, the radiance of positivity is a force that transcends individual boundaries, touching and transforming the world around us. Real-life examples from personal growth, leadership, acts of empathy, health, relationships, and social change underscore the far-reaching effects of maintaining a positive mindset. It reminds us that, in our journey through life, we have the extraordinary ability to be not only the recipients but also the bearers of the warm and illuminating light of positivity, capable of brightening the lives of those we encounter and leaving a lasting legacy of hope and inspiration.

12

Building Foundations

Learning to Swim Before Swimming Against the Tide

PSTO-12: It is often told that one must learn to swim against the tide, to be successful. Perfect. But let's remember, to do that, one must learn to swim at the first place.

In the quest for success and achievement, the metaphor of swimming against the tide is frequently invoked. It underscores the importance of resilience and determination when facing challenges. However, before one can swim against the tide, they must first learn to swim. There are a number of real-life examples from diverse fields, which portray the profound significance of mastering the basics as the foundation for success.

1. The Foundation of Education

Education is often the first step in equipping individuals with the knowledge and skills they need to navigate life's challenges. Before one can excel in any academic discipline or professional field, they must acquire a fundamental understanding of the subject matter. Consider the story of Dr. Jane Goodall, the renowned primatologist. Her groundbreaking research on chimpanzees was built upon a strong foundation in biology and natural sciences.

2. Sports and Athletics

In sports, athletes begin their journeys by mastering the fundamental skills and techniques of their chosen discipline. World-class swimmers, for instance, spend countless hours honing their strokes and building endurance in the pool before they can compete at elite levels. It's this initial dedication to the basics that forms the bedrock of their success.

3. Entrepreneurship and Business

In the world of entrepreneurship and business, aspiring leaders must first learn the fundamentals of their industry. Successful entrepreneurs often start with small ventures, learning the ins and outs of their chosen market before attempting larger and riskier endeavours. Elon Musk, for example, co-founded Zip2, an online city guide, before launching companies like Tesla and SpaceX.

4. Artistic Mastery

Artistic pursuits, too, require a deep understanding of the basics. Before creating masterpieces, painters practice their brushwork and colour theory. Musicians dedicate years to learning scales and chords. The renowned artist Pablo Picasso, known for his groundbreaking works, began his artistic journey by mastering traditional painting techniques.

5. Scientific Exploration

Even in the realm of scientific discovery, researchers start with foundational knowledge. Nobel laureates in various fields, such as physics and chemistry, often build upon existing scientific principles and theories. They must grasp the basics of their field before pushing the boundaries of knowledge.

In conclusion, the analogy of swimming against the tide beautifully illustrates the tenacity required to overcome challenges and achieve success. However, it's essential to remember that before one can swim against the tide, they must first master the art of swimming itself. Real-life examples from education, sports, entrepreneurship, the arts, and scientific exploration underscore the importance of laying a strong foundation. Mastery of the basics not only equips individuals with the skills and knowledge needed to thrive but also provides the confidence and resilience necessary to face the turbulent waters of life.

13

Nurturing Bonds Through Adversity

The True Value of Friendship

PSTO-13: Prosperity, position, status give you lots of acquaintances. Adversity brings out the friends among them to the fore. Keep investing in your friends.

In the grand theatre of life, we often find ourselves surrounded by acquaintances during times of prosperity, drawn by our status and position. Yet, it is during adversity that the true essence of friendship emerges, as genuine friends step forward to offer support and solace. In this chapter, we explore the significance of investing in and cherishing true friendships, highlighted by real-life examples that exemplify the enduring power of these bonds.

1. The Power of Solidarity in Adversity

Adversity has a unique way of revealing the authenticity of relationships. When we face challenges or difficult times, it is our true friends who stand by us, offering unwavering support and empathy. These individuals are the ones who make a tangible difference in our lives.

2. The Tale of Winston Churchill

Sir Winston Churchill, the legendary Prime Minister of the United Kingdom during World War II, faced numerous challenges and adversities in his political career. Through it all, his friend and confidant, Lord Beaverbrook, remained a steadfast source of encouragement and counsel. Beaverbrook's unwavering friendship and support played a significant role in Churchill's resilience during those tumultuous times.

3. The Band of Brothers

In the context of camaraderie and friendship forged in the crucible of adversity, the "Band of Brothers" from World War II stands as a powerful example. These soldiers, brought together by the horrors of war, formed deep bonds that lasted a lifetime. Their shared experiences created an unbreakable connection that transcended time and distance.

4. Personal Relationships and Support

In our personal lives, the importance of true friends becomes even more apparent during tough times. Whether facing a health crisis, a personal loss, or any other adversity, friends who offer emotional support, lend a listening ear, and provide a shoulder to lean on are invaluable. Their presence serves as a beacon of hope and solace.

5. The Foundation of Trust

True friendships are built on a foundation of trust and mutual understanding. During adversity, this trust is put to the test, and it is the friends who uphold their commitments and stand by us through thick and thin who prove their worth.

6. The Art of Giving and Receiving

Investing in friendships is a two-way street. Just as we receive support during adversity, we also have the privilege of being there for our friends when they need us. This reciprocal nature of friendships deepens the bonds and reinforces the idea that investing in friends is a lifelong endeavour.

In conclusion, the journey of life is marked by highs and lows, and it is in the lows that the true value of friendships becomes apparent. The examples of Winston Churchill, the "Band of Brothers," and personal relationships illustrate how genuine friends shine in times of adversity. These bonds, forged through trust, solidarity, and mutual support, are a source of strength and resilience that enrich our lives immeasurably. As we navigate the complexities of life, let us remember to invest in and cherish our friends, for they are the treasures that illuminate our darkest moments and celebrate our brightest triumphs.

14

Unconditional Love

A Key to Fulfilment in Work and Life

PSTO-14: When you love someone or something, please do so unconditionally. This applies to our work and workplace too.

Love, in its purest form, knows no conditions. It transcends expectations and flows freely, enriching our relationships and endeavours. This principle applies not only to our personal connections but also to our work and workplace. In this essay, we will explore the profound idea of unconditional love in the context of our professional lives, supported by some examples that illustrate the transformative power of this principle.

1. Love for Our Work

Unconditional love for our work is a catalyst for professional fulfilment. When we approach our tasks and responsibilities with unwavering passion and commitment, we unlock our full potential. A classic example is Steve Jobs, co-founder of Apple Inc. His deep love for design and technology drove him to create groundbreaking products like the iPhone and the Macintosh computer. His unrelenting dedication to his work not only revolutionized industries but also inspired countless individuals to pursue their passions with the same fervour.

2. The Impact of Unconditional Love in Teams

In a workplace, a culture of unconditional love and support among team members fosters collaboration, innovation, and success. When individuals genuinely care for their colleagues and their well-being, they create an environment where everyone can thrive. For instance, in Pixar Animation Studios, the commitment to nurturing a culture of trust and respect has been instrumental in producing beloved animated films. The mutual trust and love among team members translate into memorable storytelling and groundbreaking animation.

3. Customers and Client Relationships

Unconditional love extends to how we treat our customers and clients. Companies that prioritize the well-being and satisfaction of their customers, even in challenging situations, build lasting relationships and brand loyalty. Zappos, an online shoe and clothing retailer, is renowned for its unwavering commitment to customer service. Their dedication to going the extra mile for customers, including free returns and 24/7 customer support, has earned them a reputation for unconditional love and exceptional customer satisfaction.

4. Unconditional Commitment

MS Dhoni's unconditional love for cricket and the Indian cricket team is well-known. Whether it was his cool-headed leadership or stepping down from captaincy when he felt the time was right, Dhoni always prioritized the team over personal accolades. His unwavering commitment to Indian cricket, even after retirement, shows his deep, unconditional love for the game and his country.

5. Love for Sports & Community

LeBron James' love for basketball and the communities he serves is reflected in his work on and off the court. His dedication to the game is unquestionable, but what stands out is his passion for uplifting the communities through his charity work. His "I PROMISE" school initiative shows that his love for basketball transcends into a broader love for empowering the youth, demonstrating an unconditional approach to both his profession and philanthropy.

In conclusion, the concept of unconditional love is a guiding principle that transcends boundaries and enriches all aspects of our lives, including our work and workplace. Real-life examples from the worlds of business, creativity, teamwork, customer service, and personal growth demonstrate the transformative impact of approaching our endeavours with love and commitment. By fostering unconditional love in our professional lives, we not only achieve greater success and satisfaction but also create a ripple effect of positivity and inspiration that elevates our workplaces and the world around us.

15

Harnessing the Power of Positivity

Radiating Good Vibes in Your Ecosystem

PSTO-15: Vibes are all around us. It is incumbent on us to detect those positive ones and radiate it around our ecosystem.

In the intricate web of life, energy and vibrations surround us constantly. These vibes, whether positive or negative, influence our experiences and interactions with the world. It is our prerogative to discern and embrace the positive vibrations and, in turn, radiate them throughout our ecosystem. Several real-life examples showcase the transformative power of good vibes and the profound impact of positivity.

1. The Ripple Effect of Positivity

Positive energy is contagious. When we emanate good vibes, they have a ripple effect that extends far beyond our immediate interactions. Think of Mahatma Gandhi, whose unwavering commitment to nonviolence and peace radiated positive energy throughout the Indian independence movement. His peaceful protests and dedication inspired millions and ultimately led to India's independence from British rule.

2. Creating a Positive Workplace Culture

In the workplace, leaders who cultivate a culture of positivity foster innovation, collaboration, and job satisfaction. Google is a prime example of a company that prioritizes positive vibes in its work environment. The company's unique approach to employee well-being includes perks like free gourmet meals, creative workspaces, and a focus on work-life balance. This commitment to fostering positive vibes has made Google one of the most desirable places to work.

3. Spreading Kindness and Compassion

Acts of kindness and compassion are potent vehicles for positive vibes. When we extend a helping hand or offer words of encouragement, we create a domino effect of positivity. The global movement known as "Random Acts of Kindness" exemplifies this principle. It encourages individuals to perform small acts of kindness, such as buying a coffee for a stranger or leaving an uplifting note, with the aim of spreading positivity and brightening someone's day.

4. Nurturing Positive Relationships

Positive vibes are instrumental in nurturing meaningful relationships. When we approach our interactions with authenticity, empathy, and respect, we strengthen our connections with others. Consider the enduring friendship between Fred Rogers, the beloved host of "Mister Rogers' Neighbourhood," and François Clemmons, who played Officer Clemmons on the show. Their friendship, based on mutual respect and genuine care, radiated positivity and inspired viewers of all ages.

5. Spreading Joy through Philanthropy

Radiating positive vibes across your ecosystem can always start with philanthropic initiative. Let's take the case of Dolly Parton.

Dolly Parton, the iconic country singer and actress, is not only known for her music but also for her philanthropic efforts. Her "Imagination Library" program has provided millions of free books to children, fostering a love of reading and education. Her unwavering commitment to spreading joy and positivity has had a profound impact on countless families.

In conclusion, the awareness and cultivation of positive vibes are essential components of a fulfilling and harmonious life. Real-life examples from leadership, workplace culture, acts of kindness, relationships, and spreading joy through philanthropy underscore the transformative power of embracing and radiating positivity. As we navigate the complexities of our interconnected world, let us remember that our ability to detect and amplify positive vibes is a gift that can elevate our ecosystem and inspire positive change on a grand scale. By being beacons of positivity, we contribute to the betterment of our communities, workplaces, and the world at large, leaving a lasting legacy of warmth and inspiration.

16

The Fickle Nature of Fame

Preparing for the Inevitable Changes

PSTO-16: You keep on accumulating crowds cheering for you, on your way up. But you must realise that like everything else in life, this is also temporary. Keep yourself suitably prepared.

In the pursuit of success, especially in the public eye, individuals often experience the adulation of crowds and the euphoria of fame. However, it is crucial to recognize that like all aspects of life, this too is transient. We must remain aware of the ephemeral nature of fame. The importance of preparing oneself for the inevitable changes is well demonstrated by real-life examples from various domains.

1. The Rise and Fall of Pop Icons

In the world of entertainment, pop icons frequently experience meteoric rises to stardom, with legions of adoring fans cheering their every move. Yet, history has shown that fame can be fleeting. For instance, consider the rise and fall of pop stars like Britney Spears and Justin Bieber, who both experienced immense fame at a young age. While they continue to have successful careers, they also navigated periods of intense public scrutiny and personal challenges. Their stories remind us of the unpredictable nature of fame and the need for resilience.

2. The Ebb and Flow of Sports Glory

In the realm of sports, athletes often bask in the glory of victories and the admiration of fans. However, injuries, performance slumps, or shifts in public sentiment can quickly change the landscape. Tennis legend Serena Williams, despite her incredible success, has faced setbacks and injuries during her career. Her ability to persevere and adapt exemplifies the importance of being prepared for the highs and lows of fame.

3. The Business World's Roller Coaster

In the business world, entrepreneurs and CEOs may experience periods of skyrocketing success and acclaim. However, market dynamics, economic fluctuations, and competition can lead to abrupt changes. Take the example of former Theranos CEO Elizabeth Holmes. Once hailed as a visionary entrepreneur, she faced a high-profile scandal and legal troubles that dramatically altered her public image.

4. The Volatile World of Politics

Political leaders, too, are not immune to the changing tides of public opinion. They may ride waves of popularity, only to encounter challenging times that test their resilience and adaptability. Former President Barack Obama, for instance, navigated the complexities of the U.S. political landscape, with both soaring approval ratings and periods of intense criticism. His ability to maintain composure and leadership during changing circumstances serves as a model for political adaptability.

5. The Importance of Preparation

The key takeaway from these examples is the importance of

preparation for the uncertainties of fame and success. Being mentally and emotionally equipped to handle both adoration and criticism is crucial. Developing a strong support network, cultivating resilience, and staying true to one's values can help individuals weather the changes that fame brings.

In conclusion, the allure of fame can be intoxicating, but it is essential to recognize its transient nature. Real-life examples from entertainment, sports, business, and politics emphasize the unpredictability of public sentiment and the need for preparedness. As individuals ascend the ladder of success, they must equip themselves with the emotional fortitude and adaptability to navigate the inevitable changes that come with fame. By doing so, they can maintain their authenticity and continue to make meaningful contributions to their respective fields, regardless of the shifting winds of public opinion.

17

The Wisdom of Balance

Observing and Listening Before Speaking

PSTO-17: It's rightly told that Almighty has given us two eyes to observe more, two ears to listen more, but one mouth to speak less. Sooner we realise it and implement it, better it is for us.

The fact that we have been endowed with two eyes to observe more, two ears to listen more, and just one mouth to speak less holds a great value to each one of us in life. It speaks of the importance of balanced communication and the virtues of keen observation and active listening. The significance of this thought is well supported by various real-life examples that illustrate the transformative power of observing and listening before speaking.

1. The Power of Observation

Observation is the gateway to understanding the world around us. By keenly observing our surroundings, we gain valuable insights into people, situations, and the nuances of life. The life of famous naturalist Charles Darwin serves as an exemplary model of observation. His meticulous observations of various species during his voyage on the HMS Beagle were instrumental in the development of his groundbreaking theory of evolution.

2. Learning by simple Observing

Sachin Tendulkar's legendary status in cricket came not just from his talent but also from his ability to observe and listen more than he spoke. His humble demeanor, despite his global fame, showed that he believed in letting his work do the talking. He spent a lot of time learning from teammates, coaches, and competitors, a trait that allowed him to continue evolving as a cricketer throughout his career.

3. Effective Leadership and Decision-making

In leadership and decision-making, the ability to observe and listen before speaking is paramount. Leaders who take the time to gather information, consider diverse perspectives, and assess the implications of their choices make more informed and effective decisions. Warren Buffett, one of the most successful investors in history, is known for his patient and deliberate approach to investing, which involves extensive observation and research before making decisions.

4. Conflict Resolution and Diplomacy

In the realm of conflict resolution and diplomacy, effective communication begins with listening. Nelson Mandela, South Africa's revered leader, exemplified the power of listening in the context of reconciliation. His willingness to engage in dialogue and listen to the concerns of all parties played a pivotal role in dismantling apartheid and establishing a more inclusive society.

5. Personal Growth and Empathy

On a personal level, embracing the principle of observing and listening before speaking fosters personal growth and empathy. When we actively seek to understand the experiences and perspectives of others, we expand our horizons and become more compassionate individuals. The writings of Maya Angelou, for instance, are steeped in empathy and an acute awareness of human experiences, reflecting her profound ability to observe and listen deeply.

In conclusion, the wisdom encapsulated in the saying about our two eyes, two ears, and one mouth is a reminder of the importance of balanced communication and the virtues of observation and active listening. Real-life examples from the realms of science, empathy, leadership, diplomacy, and personal growth underscore the transformative power of this principle. By embracing this wisdom, we can enhance our understanding of the world, forge deeper connections with others, and make more informed and empathetic decisions. Ultimately, it is through observing and listening that we can strive for greater harmony, compassion, and wisdom in our interactions with the world and the people in it.

18

The Alchemy of Leadership

Transforming Individuals into a Dream Team

PSTO-18: Choosing a team of your own choice is the dream of any leader. But converting any team member one gets to a team member of your choice, is the sign of a great team leader.

Leadership is often associated with the ability to choose one's team, but the true mark of a great team leader lies in the skill to mould and inspire any group of individuals into a cohesive and high-performing team. The idea that exceptional leaders can transform team members into their ideal collaborators gets resonance in many real-life examples from various fields.

1. Sir Alex Ferguson's Legacy in Soccer

Sir Alex Ferguson, the legendary manager of Manchester United Football Club, is celebrated not just for his ability to assemble star-studded teams but also for his knack for transforming young and unproven players into world-class talent. He was renowned for his mentorship and ability to instil a sense of unity and purpose in his teams. Under his leadership, Manchester United became one of the most successful soccer clubs in history.

2. Building the U.S. Space Program

The U.S. space program, particularly the Apollo missions that landed the first humans on the moon, serves as another remarkable example. NASA's team leaders, including figures like Gene Kranz and Chris Kraft, faced the daunting challenge of orchestrating complex missions involving hundreds of individuals from diverse backgrounds. They succeeded not by handpicking ideal teams but by fostering a culture of collaboration, innovation, and shared vision.

3. Jacinda Ardern's exemplary leadership as PM, New Zealand

Jacinda Ardern's leadership as the Prime Minister of New Zealand is characterized by empathy and unity. Her effective response to crises, such as the Christchurch mosque shootings and the COVID-19 pandemic, exemplifies her ability to bring diverse individuals and communities together to achieve common goals. Through her humane approach, not only she converted her team, but almost the entire country into a winning team during crisis.

4. Being a 'Student of the Game' – Bill Belichick

Often considered as a person who understood the American football to the core and transformed individual players into a cohesive unit, Bill Belichick, the head coach of the New England Patriots in the NFL, has transformed his team into a dynasty. His leadership and strategic thinking have consistently turned individual talents into a cohesive unit that has won multiple Super Bowl titles, emphasizing teamwork and discipline.

In conclusion, while choosing a team of one's own choice can be a leader's dream, the ability to convert any team members into ideal collaborators is a hallmark of exceptional leadership. Real-life examples from the world of sports, space exploration, technology, education, and politics illustrate the transformative power of leadership in shaping teams. Great leaders inspire, mentor, and unite individuals, unlocking their full potential and enabling them to achieve remarkable feats. In doing so, they prove that leadership is not solely about the talent you inherit but about the vision, inspiration, and guidance you provide to those who look up to you.

19

Embracing the Beauty of the World

Breaking Free from Our Silos

PSTO-19: World is so beautiful. We have to simply come out of our silos, our cocoons and look around. There will never be a dull moment anymore.

The world we inhabit is a wondrous tapestry of diversity, teeming with beauty and opportunities waiting to be explored. Yet, too often, we confine ourselves to our comfort zones and routines, missing out on the richness of life that surrounds us. In this chapter, we will delve into the idea of breaking free from our silos and embracing the world's beauty, well supported by some examples that illuminate the profound impact of this choice.

1. Finding Beauty in Simple Things

Ruskin Bond, the renowned Indian author, has spent decades writing about the beauty of the world around him, especially in the small, everyday moments of life in the hills. Bond's ability to observe and appreciate nature, people, and life in all its forms shows the joy that can come from stepping out of one's cocoon and seeing the world with fresh eyes.

2. Exploring the World Beyond Active Innings

Usain Bolt, the fastest man on earth, has taken the opportunity to explore life beyond the track after retirement. Embracing travel, music, and new experiences, Bolt demonstrates how stepping out of the narrow focus of athletics has allowed him to experience the world's beauty in different forms. His post-athletic life is filled with vibrancy, showing that there's always something new to appreciate once we step outside our silos.

3. The Joys of Cultural Exchange

Breaking free from our silos also means engaging with different cultures and people. Through cultural exchange programs like the Peace Corps, individuals immerse themselves in new communities, fostering mutual understanding and appreciation. These experiences not only broaden their horizons but also enrich their lives with lasting friendships and cultural insights.

4. Stepping Beyond the Traditional Role

Sudha Murthy stepped beyond the traditional role of a computer scientist and corporate leader when she dedicated her life to philanthropic work. Though she had a successful career, she chose to explore the world of literature and social service, impacting rural education, healthcare, and public libraries in India. By coming out of her corporate cocoon, she found deeper purpose and beauty in helping others, eventually becoming a beloved author and a force for social good.

In conclusion, the world is a treasure trove of beauty, waiting for us to step out of our silos and embrace it. Real-life examples from travel, nature, cultural exchange, and the arts work illustrate the transformative power of exploring the world around us. By breaking free from our self-imposed limitations and seeking out the wonders of the world, we not only enrich our own lives but also contribute to a more interconnected and harmonious global community. Each moment becomes a source of inspiration and wonder, ensuring that there will never be a dull moment again as we embrace the beauty of our world.

20

The Power of Pause

Finding Clarity and Creativity in Moments of Doubt

PSTO-20: Whenever in doubt, just pause, take a deep breath and think. You will be flooded with ideas/options

Life is full of complex decisions and moments of uncertainty. In these times of doubt, the simple act of pausing, taking a deep breath, and allowing our thoughts to flow can be transformative. There are examples galore in the real-life which highlight the remarkable ideas and options that emerge when we pause and reflect.

1. Well-being and Mindful Leadership

Arianna Huffington, the co-founder of The Huffington Post and founder of Thrive Global, is an advocate for well-being and mindful leadership. After experiencing burnout, she paused to reflect on the importance of sleep, stress reduction, and personal wellness. Her pause led to the creation of Thrive Global, a platform dedicated to helping individuals and organizations achieve well-being and productivity.

2. Decision-making and Clarity

When faced with complex decisions, taking a moment to pause and reflect can lead to clarity and better choices. Warren Buffett, one of the most successful investors in history, is known for his deliberate and thoughtful decision-making process. He often takes his time to consider all angles before making investment decisions, allowing him to navigate the complexities of the financial world with remarkable precision.

3. The Art of Leadership

Effective leaders understand the importance of pausing to assess situations and make informed decisions. Former U.S. President Abraham Lincoln was known for his thoughtful leadership during one of the most tumultuous periods in American history, the Civil War. His ability to pause, reflect, and make critical decisions was instrumental in guiding the nation through its darkest days.

4. The Entrepreneurial Pause

On a personal level, pausing to reflect is a gateway to self-discovery and personal growth. Many entrepreneurs do it. Let's take example of Richard Branson, the maverick owner of the Virgin group. As per his own admission, he frequently takes breaks from his busy schedule to recharge and brainstorm new ideas. He believes that these pauses are essential for maintaining creativity and innovation in his businesses.

In conclusion, the practice of pausing, taking a deep breath, and allowing our thoughts to flow is a profound tool for finding clarity, creativity, and solutions in moments of doubt. Real-life examples from the realms of creativity, decision-making, mindfulness, and leadership illustrate the transformative power of this practice. By embracing the wisdom of pause, we can navigate life's uncertainties with grace and discover a wellspring of ideas and options that empower us to make informed choices and lead fulfilling lives.

21

Life is a Shared Story

Embracing Openness, Learning, and Enrichment

PSTO-21: Life should be like an open book. We should allow people to access it, gain from it as well as contribute in a way to make the book richer.

Life is a tapestry of experiences, lessons, and stories waiting to be shared. Rather than keeping our life's locked away, we have the opportunity to let others access our book and contribute to its richness. The idea that life should be like an open book is amply demonstrated in life that illustrate the profound impact of sharing and learning from one another.

1. The Wisdom of Generations

Across generations, there is a wealth of knowledge, experiences, and wisdom that can be passed down like chapters in an open book. Grandparents, for instance, hold valuable life lessons and stories that can enrich the lives of their grandchildren. Through storytelling and shared experiences, younger generations can gain from the wisdom of their elders and contribute their fresh perspectives to the family narrative.

2. The Power of Mentorship

Mentorship is a powerful form of sharing and learning. Seasoned professionals and experts often take on mentees, providing guidance and insights to help them navigate their careers and life journeys. For example, Sheryl Sandberg, the COO of Facebook, has been an advocate for mentorship and has mentored numerous individuals, including Mark Zuckerberg. Her mentorship has played a role in shaping the next generation of leaders.

3. The Beauty of Cultural Exchange

Cultural exchange is like turning the pages of a global open book. Traveling and immersing oneself in different cultures allows us to access and contribute to the diversity of human experiences. Programs like the Fulbright Scholar Program enable individuals to share their knowledge and culture while gaining insights into others' lives, fostering mutual understanding and enrichment.

4. The Impact of Autobiographies and Memoirs

Many individuals choose to open their own life books by sharing their personal stories through autobiographies and memoirs. The memoir "Educated" by Tara Westover, for instance, invites readers into the author's remarkable journey from growing up in a strict and isolated household to pursuing education at prestigious institutions. Her openness in sharing her experiences has touched and inspired countless readers. "My life in Full" by Indra Nooyi, published in 2021 is one more such example, which can certainly inspire hundreds of women executives around the world.

5. Online Communities and Social Media

In the digital age, online communities and social media platforms provide opportunities for individuals to share their life experiences, expertise, and stories on a global scale. Bloggers, vloggers, and content creators share their passions and life adventures, fostering connections and enriching the lives of their audiences.

6. The Spirit of Volunteering

Volunteering is a tangible way to contribute to the open book of life. When individuals volunteer their time and skills to support causes and communities, they not only give back but also learn from the experiences of those they serve. The work of volunteers in organizations like Habitat for Humanity exemplifies the spirit of shared contributions and enrichment.

In conclusion, life as an open book is a metaphor for the beauty of sharing, learning, and contributing to the collective human experience. Real-life examples from family traditions, mentorship, cultural exchange, literature, online communities, and volunteering illustrate the profound impact of embracing an open-book approach to life. By allowing others to access our stories and experiences and by actively seeking to learn from others, we create a world where the book of life is continuously enriched, and the boundaries of understanding and empathy are expanded. In this open-book world, each individual becomes a co-author of a richer and more interconnected human narrative.

22

Mastering the Art of Time

Harness Every Moment for Meaningful Living

PSTO-22: We all know 'time and tide wait for none'. But making the time work for us is in our hands. We can make every moment count.

The relentless march of time is an undeniable fact of life, and the saying, "Time and tide wait for none," serves as a constant reminder of its unforgiving nature. However, the power to make time work for us is firmly within our grasp. In this chapter, we will explore the notion that every moment can be made to count and provide examples that illustrate the transformative potential of this mindset.

1. The Value of Time Management

Effective time management is the cornerstone of making time work for us. Consider the story of Elon Musk, CEO of SpaceX and Tesla. He manages a multitude of demanding responsibilities, from leading cutting-edge companies to exploring the frontiers of space travel. Musk's meticulous time management skills enable him to juggle these endeavours successfully, making the most of every moment.

2. Time Management despite Adversity

Aung San Suu Kyi, a Burmese politician and Nobel Peace Prize winner, spent years under house arrest for her pro-democracy activism. Still, that did not deter her from continuing with her fight. Despite the challenges she faced, she harnessed her time to advocate for human rights and democracy in Myanmar.

3. Lifelong Learning and Growth

The commitment to continuous learning and personal growth ensures that each moment contributes to our development. Richard Branson, the founder of Virgin Group, is known for his adventurous spirit and willingness to embrace new challenges. His dedication to learning and pushing boundaries has allowed him to expand his business empire while relishing every opportunity for personal and professional growth.

4. Acts of Kindness and Service

Acts of kindness and service to others are timeless ways to make each moment meaningful. The story of Mother Teresa, who dedicated her life to helping the poorest of the poor, exemplifies this principle. Her simple acts of compassion, whether caring for the sick or providing for the destitute, transformed countless lives and made every moment she lived truly count.

5. Seizing every Opportunity

Anand Mahindra, the chairman of Mahindra Group, is known for making the most of every moment. From expanding Mahindra's footprint globally to embracing digital transformation, Mahindra's career demonstrates his belief in maximizing the potential of time. He has turned many business challenges into opportunities, understanding that waiting is not an option in a fast-paced world, and every moment is an opportunity for growth.

In conclusion, the adage "Time and tide wait for none" may remind us of the inevitability of time's passage, but the ability to make time work for us is entirely within our control. Real-life examples from the realms of time management, pursuing passion, lifelong learning, acts of kindness, and seizing opportunity illustrate the transformative power of this mindset. By consciously choosing to invest our time in meaningful pursuits, we not only make each moment count for ourselves but also leave a lasting legacy of positive change and inspiration in the world. The key lies in recognizing that time is a precious resource and using it wisely to shape a life of purpose and impact.

23

The Power of One

Making a Difference, One Life at a Time

PSTO-23: It's often asked, what can I do alone? Yes you can do. If we can individually make a difference to one single life, that itself is a big step. Let's resolve to do that, NOW.

In a world filled with complex challenges and seemingly insurmountable problems, it's common to wonder, "What can I do alone?" The answer is profound: you can make a significant difference in the life of just one person. Let us explore the notion that impacting a single life can be a catalyst for positive change and provide some examples that illustrate the transformative power of this simple yet profound act.

1. Bringing Peace, Single-handedly

Didier Drogba, the legendary Ivorian footballer, played a critical role in bringing peace to his war-torn country, Côte d'Ivoire. His single act of pleading for a ceasefire after his team qualified for the 2006 World Cup had a massive impact on the country, helping to end the civil war. Drogba's actions show that even one person, especially one in a position of influence, can bring about meaningful change.

2. Innovating the Education

Sonam Wangchuk, an engineer and innovator from Ladakh, made a significant difference in the lives of young students through his solo efforts. He started the Students' Educational and Cultural Movement of Ladakh (SECMOL) to reform the education system in the region. By focusing on practical, culturally relevant education, Wangchuk transformed the future of thousands of children, showing how one person can bring about lasting change through individual actions.

3. Empowering Through Knowledge

Srinivasa Ramanujan, a self-taught Indian mathematician, exemplifies empowerment through knowledge. Despite limited resources and formal education, his passion, dedication, and thirst for knowledge drove him to make groundbreaking contributions to mathematics. Seeking mentorship and global recognition, he overcame adversity, leaving an enduring legacy that inspires others. Ramanujan's story highlights how education, fuelled by determination, empowers individuals to overcome obstacles and make a lasting impact.

4. Humanitarian Aid in Crisis

In times of crisis and natural disasters, humanitarian organizations and individuals often come together to provide aid and relief. The work of individual volunteers in organizations like Doctors Without Borders showcases how one person's dedication and expertise can save lives and provide hope in the face of adversity.

In conclusion, the belief that "If we can individually make a difference to one single life, that itself is a big step" is a testament to the profound impact of our actions. Real-life examples from acts of kindness, mentorship, education, and humanitarian aid illustrate the transformative power of touching just one life. By resolving to make a difference in the life of another, we not only bring positive change to that person but also contribute to a world where empathy, kindness, and compassion prevail. The key lies in recognizing the potential of our actions, no matter how small, to create meaningful and lasting change in the lives of others.

24

Seizing the Present

The Art of Living in the Now

PSTO-24: We must not brood over the past, nor worry about the future. We may learn from the past, to make our future better. But we must thrive to live in the present. That is most important.

The human mind often wanders between the past and the future, dwelling on regrets and worries. However, the true essence of life lies in the present moment. We must not brood over the past, nor worry about the future; instead, we should strive to live in the present. Real-life examples illustrate the profound significance of embracing the here and now.

1. The Art of Mindfulness

Rohit Sharma's journey from the heartbreak of losing the World Cup final against Australia at home to lifting the T20 World Cup is a powerful example of learning from the past while thriving in the present. After India's painful defeat in the 2023 ODI World Cup final at home, there was immense disappointment and scrutiny over the team's performance. Rohit, as the captain, faced a lot of criticism. However, rather than brooding over the loss, he chose to reflect on the lessons learned from the defeat. He recognized that dwelling on the past wouldn't change the outcome but improving the team's mindset and strategy could pave the way for future success. With a renewed focus, he led India into the T20 World Cup with determination and a clear vision. He utilized the past experience to guide the team, tweaking their approach and instilling a sense of belief. Rohit inspired his team to play with confidence and resilience. Ultimately, his leadership and present-focused mindset culminated in India lifting the T20 World Cup trophy.

2. Athletic Excellence

Athletes often excel when they are completely in the zone, fully focused on the task at hand. Michael Phelps, the legendary Olympic swimmer, is a prime example. His ability to immerse himself in the present moment during races contributed to his record-breaking achievements. By blocking out distractions and concentrating on the present, he achieved his extraordinary success.

3. Creative Inspiration

Artists, writers, and musicians often draw their inspiration from the present moment. Georgia O'Keeffe, the renowned American artist, found inspiration in the details of everyday life. Her ability to capture the beauty of the present, whether through close-up flowers or expansive landscapes, continues to resonate with audiences around the world.

4. Humanitarian Acts of Kindness

Humanitarian work often involves responding to immediate needs in crisis situations. Dr. Paul Farmer, co-founder of Partners In Health, is a physician and anthropologist who has dedicated his life to providing healthcare to impoverished communities. His work demonstrates the importance of being present and responsive to the urgent needs of others.

In conclusion, the past and future are important aspects of our lives, but the true richness of existence lies in living fully in the present. Real-life examples from games, athletics, the arts, and humanitarian work illustrate the transformative power of being present. By embracing the present moment, we can find clarity, creativity, and a deeper connection to our own lives and the lives of others. It is in the now that we have the opportunity to shape our future and learn from our past, making each moment a precious gift to be treasured and lived to the fullest.

25

The Journey of Self-Love

A Path to Loving Others

PSTO-25: We should learn to love ourselves well enough so that we can love all around us. Again for loving ourselves, we must know ourselves well too.

The essence of love radiates from within, and to truly love others, we must first learn to love ourselves. This chapter explores the idea that self-love is the foundation upon which our capacity to love others is built. It emphasizes the importance of self-awareness as a precursor to self-love and provides real-life examples that illustrate the transformative power of this journey.

1. Self-Awareness: The First Step to Self-Love

Before we can love ourselves, we must first know ourselves. Self-awareness is the key to understanding our strengths, weaknesses, values, and desires. Psychologist Carl Rogers emphasized the importance of self-actualization, a process that involves becoming more self-aware and authentic. By gaining insights into our true selves, we lay the groundwork for self-love.

2. The Healing Power of Self-compassion

Self-compassion is an integral aspect of self-love. Dr. Kristin Neff, a leading researcher on self-compassion, advocates for treating ourselves with the same kindness and understanding that we would offer to a friend in times of suffering or failure. This practice of self-compassion nurtures self-love and allows us to extend compassion to others more readily.

3. Parenting with Love and Empathy

Parents who cultivate self-love in themselves can model it for their children. The work of Dr. Laura Markham, a psychologist and parenting expert, highlights the importance of positive parenting practices rooted in empathy and self-awareness. By practicing self-love, parents create a loving environment that fosters their children's emotional well-being.

4. The Power of Acceptance and Resilience

Self-love is closely intertwined with self-acceptance and resilience. Dr. Brené Brown, a research professor and author, explores the transformative effects of vulnerability, authenticity, and self-compassion. Her work has inspired countless individuals to embrace their imperfections, thereby nurturing self-love and fostering more meaningful connections with others.

5. Acts of Kindness and Generosity

The power of self-love leading to a deep love for humanity is exemplified in the life of Dr. A.P.J. Abdul Kalam, former President of India. Known as the "People's President" and the "Missile Man of India," Dr. Kalam's unwavering self-belief and love for self-improvement propelled him from a modest background to the highest office in the land. His humility, kindness, and genuine concern for the well-being of his fellow citizens demonstrated that a strong sense of self-worth can fuel a profound love for humanity. Dr.

Kalam's legacy lies not only in his scientific achievements but in his ability to inspire and uplift people of all backgrounds, emphasizing that self-love can be a catalyst for spreading love and compassion to the wider world.

In conclusion, the journey of self-love is a transformative path that allows us to radiate love and compassion to all those around us. Real-life examples from psychology, parenting, resilience research, and historical leadership demonstrate the profound impact of self-love on our ability to love others. By understanding and embracing our true selves, practicing self-compassion, and nurturing self-acceptance, we not only cultivate a deeper sense of self-love but also become beacons of love, empathy, and kindness in our relationships and communities. It is in the richness of self-love that we find the capacity to create a world overflowing with love for all.

26

The Journey of Resilience

Transforming Life's Set-backs into Strength

PSTO-26: We have one life. A personal jolt, here and there, should not deter us from going forward. Rather, it should galvanize us to be more refined and a much better human being.

Life is an unpredictable journey, filled with moments that can jolt us off our course. However, it is our response to these jolts that defines our character and shapes our path. This chapter explores the idea that despite life's challenges, we have one life to live, and every set-back we encounter can be an opportunity for personal growth and transformation. Real-life examples do illustrate the power of resilience and refinement in the face of adversity.

1. Overcoming Personal Tragedy

Tragedy can strike unexpectedly, leaving us devastated. Yet, many individuals have turned their personal tragedies into a source of strength and inspiration. Oprah Winfrey, for instance, faced a challenging upbringing marked by poverty and abuse. However, she channelled her experiences into a successful career as a media mogul, philanthropist, and advocate for personal growth.

2. The Resilience of Deepa Malik

Resilience indeed plays a pivotal role in transforming setbacks into remarkable comebacks, and Deepa Malik, the Indian para-athlete, exemplifies this with unwavering determination. Paralyzed from the waist down due to a spinal tumor, Deepa refused to let her disability define her life. Instead, she embraced a path of relentless resilience and reinvention. Deepa's journey to becoming an accomplished para-athlete, clinching numerous medals and accolades, including a silver at the Paralympics, demonstrated her unyielding spirit. Her ability to overcome physical limitations, adapt to adversity, and achieve success in the face of daunting setbacks showcases the extraordinary power of resilience in forging extraordinary comebacks.

3. Turning Setbacks into Comebacks

In the early 2000s, Amitabh Bachchan was facing a lull in his acting career, with a series of flops. The period was marked by acute financial challenges too. However, in 2000, he took a bold step by agreeing to host the Indian version of the popular quiz show "Who Wants to Be a Millionaire," known as "Kaun Banega Crorepati." His charismatic and authoritative presence on the show struck a chord with the Indian audience. His rich baritone voice and his empathetic engagement with contestants connected with viewers on a personal level. His charm and intelligence made KBC an instant hit, and it soon became one of the most-watched television programs in India. The success of "Kaun Banega Crorepati" marked a significant turning point in Amitabh Bachchan's career. It not only revived his popularity but also established him as a versatile entertainer in both the film and television industries. His comeback with KBC showcased his ability to adapt to new challenges and reinvent himself, proving that setbacks can be transformed into remarkable comebacks.

4. Overcoming Setbacks

Mary Kom's boxing career is a testament to her resilience. Despite facing several personal and professional setbacks, including balancing motherhood with her sport, she continued to excel. Her ability to bounce back from challenges has made her a more determined and refined athlete, inspiring countless people with her grit and perseverance.

In conclusion, life's jolts, whether personal tragedies, adversity, health challenges, setbacks, or financial hardships, are opportunities for resilience and refinement. Real-life examples from the worlds of media, politics, entertainment, science, and literature illustrate the remarkable capacity of individuals to overcome adversity and emerge as refined and better human beings. The key lies in embracing these challenges as opportunities for growth, learning, and personal development. Instead of allowing life's jolts to deter us, we can use them as catalysts for becoming stronger, more compassionate, and more resilient individuals. In doing so, we not only navigate life's uncertainties with grace but also inspire others to embark on their own journeys of transformation and self-improvement.

27

The Art of Meaningful Journeys

Enriching the Path to Achieving Goals

PSTO-27: Goals are very important. But the journey to reach the Goal is much more important. We must enrich the journey by making it more meaningful, not only individually for us, but for our fellow travellers also.

In the pursuit of our goals, it's easy to become fixated on the destination and overlook the significance of the journey itself. This chapter explores the idea that while goals are important, the journey to reach them holds even greater value. It emphasizes the importance of enriching this journey, not only for our individual growth but also for the benefit of our fellow travellers. Real-life examples illuminate the transformative power of making the journey meaningful.

1. Empowering others

Enriching the path to achieving the team's goals is exemplified by the illustrious career of M.S. Dhoni, the former captain of the Indian cricket team. Dhoni's success was not just defined by his on-field achievements but also by his unique leadership style. He enriched the journey for each member by fostering a harmonious team environment, showcasing calmness under pressure, and cultivating young talent. His focus on building a legacy beyond personal records and his ability to blend leadership with humility demonstrate that the path to reaching goals can be more fulfilling when it includes empowering others and leaving a lasting impact beyond individual accomplishments.

2. Acts of Kindness Along the Way

In bustling cities, where daily commutes can be stressful, there's a heartwarming trend of "subway therapy." Commuters leave encouraging notes, inspirational quotes, or small gifts for fellow travellers to discover during their journeys. These acts of kindness brighten the often hectic and impersonal commute. For instance, a tired office worker might find a note that says, "You've got this!" on a particularly rough morning. Such simple gestures remind people of the goodness in humanity and create a sense of camaraderie among strangers. The "subway therapy" movement showcases how small acts of kindness can enhance our daily routines and infuse positivity into the most mundane aspects of life. It demonstrates that a little compassion can go a long way in making the world a better place, one subway ride at a time.

3. Focussing on the Journey

Vijay Amritraj, one of India's most celebrated tennis players, beautifully exemplifies this philosophy. While he had clear goals of excelling in tennis and representing India on the global stage, he always focused on the journey and how he could enrich it for others along the way.

4. Collaboration and Teamwork

Collaboration and teamwork are integral to enriching the journey, especially in professional and organizational contexts. The success of NASA's Apollo 11 mission to the moon is a testament to the power of teamwork. The collective efforts of scientists, engineers, astronauts, and countless others enriched the journey to achieve this historic goal.

In conclusion, while goals provide direction and purpose in our lives, the journey to reach them offers a wealth of opportunities for growth, kindness, mentorship, collaboration, and leadership. Real-life examples illustrate the transformative power of enriching the journey. By embracing the idea that the journey is as important as the destination, we not only find greater fulfilment and meaning in our own lives but also contribute to a world where the paths we travel are filled with shared experiences, personal growth, and positive impacts on those who journey alongside us. Ultimately, it is in the enrichment of the journey that we discover the true essence of achievement and fulfilment.

28

It's All Our Business

The Power of Responding Positively to the World Around Us

PSTO-28: Many a time, we ignore events around us as, 'None of my business'. But when the same happens to us, we feel hurt that no one cared. In nutshell, everything happening around us is our business. Respond to it positively.

In our busy lives, it's easy to adopt the mindset of "None of my business" when it comes to events happening around us. However, this chapter explores the idea that everything happening around us is, in fact, our business, and responding positively to these events can lead to a more connected and compassionate world. Real-life examples light up the transformative power of embracing this perspective.

1. Acts of Kindness and Compassion

Acts of kindness and compassion often begin with acknowledging that everything around us is our business. The story of Nicholas Winton, who rescued 669 children from the Holocaust, is a prime example. Winton's intervention was sparked by a sense of responsibility and compassion when he saw the plight of refugee children. His actions demonstrated that responding positively to the suffering of others can lead to remarkable acts of kindness.

2. Advocating for Social Change

Aamir Khan, a prominent Indian actor, has utilized his platform to address social issues through his films and television show "Satyamev Jayate." Rather than ignoring societal problems, he actively engages with them, raising awareness about topics like child labor, domestic violence, and education. By stepping into the "business" of social issues, Khan not only highlights the importance of caring for others but also inspires his audience to respond positively and take action.

3. Environmental Stewardship

Taking responsibility for our environment is another example of responding positively to events around us. Greta Thunberg, a young climate activist, responded to the climate crisis by initiating the "Fridays for Future" movement. Her actions have inspired millions worldwide to address the urgent issue of climate change.

4. Advocacy for Marginal Communities

Dr. Binayak Sen, a human rights activist and paediatrician, saw the suffering of tribal communities in Chhattisgarh as his business, even though it wasn't directly affecting him. He spoke out against state violence, advocated for the rights of these marginalized communities, and provided healthcare in areas where none existed. His belief that injustice anywhere is everyone's responsibility led him to become a vocal advocate for the voiceless.

5. Humanitarian Efforts

Harish Hande, founder of SELCO, saw the lack of access to electricity in rural India as his responsibility. While many might have ignored the issue as 'not their business,' Harish actively pursued solutions to bring affordable solar energy to underserved areas. His approach helped uplift rural communities by providing them with sustainable energy solutions, improving their quality of life.

In conclusion, the notion that everything happening around us is our business is a powerful perspective that fosters kindness, compassion, and positive action. Examples from acts of kindness, community engagement, environmental stewardship, advocacy for social change, and humanitarian efforts illustrate the transformative power of embracing this mindset. By responding positively to events around us, we not only create a more connected and compassionate world but also contribute to positive change on both a local and global scale. It is in recognizing our interconnectedness and taking responsibility for the well-being of others that we truly become agents of positive change and progress.

29

The Power of Acknowledgment

Fostering a Motivated Ecosystem

PSTO-29: We must learn to give credit whenever or wherever it is due. But giving credits, where it may not be very clearly due, should also be encouraged. We may thus create a motivated ecosystem. An investment for future. Isn't it?

In a world driven by innovation and collaboration, giving credit where it is due plays a pivotal role in fostering a motivated and supportive ecosystem. This chapter explores the idea that not only should we acknowledge contributions when they are clearly due, but we should also encourage a culture of generous recognition, even when it may not be immediately evident. Real-life examples from the fields of science and technology illuminate the transformative impact of this approach, highlighting how it can be an investment in a brighter future.

1. Scientific Collaboration and Shared Credit

The field of science thrives on collaboration, where discoveries are often the result of collective efforts. The discovery of the structure of DNA, for instance, involved the work of multiple scientists, including James Watson, Francis Crick, and Rosalind Franklin. While Watson and Crick are well-known for their contributions, acknowledging the essential work of Rosalind Franklin posthumously highlighted the importance of shared credit and a more inclusive approach to recognition.

2. Open-Source Software and Collaborative Innovation

In the tech world, open-source software development relies on collective contributions from developers worldwide. The Linux operating system is a prime example of a collaborative effort led by Linus Torvalds. The open-source community's ethos of giving credit and sharing knowledge fosters a vibrant ecosystem of innovation and collaboration.

3. Recognizing Unsung Heroes in Technology

Many technological advancements involve the contributions of numerous individuals, some of whom may remain relatively unknown. The invention of the World Wide Web, for instance, often credits Sir Tim Berners-Lee as its creator. Still, it's important to recognize the contributions of others, such as Marc Andreessen and his development of the first widely used web browser, which played a significant role in popularizing the web.

4. Inclusive Recognition in Research Teams

In research teams, it is essential to acknowledge the collective effort rather than just singling out one individual. The successful landing of the Mars rover Perseverance, for example, involved the work of thousands of scientists and engineers at NASA's Jet Propulsion Laboratory. The inclusive recognition of the entire team's dedication and expertise showcases the value of acknowledging contributions broadly.

5. Encouraging Innovation through Inclusive Patents

In the field of technology, patents often represent the culmination of collaborative efforts. Tesla, the electric car company, made headlines by opening its electric vehicle patents to the public. By sharing their innovations, Tesla aimed to encourage and accelerate the development of sustainable transportation technologies, demonstrating the power of generous recognition in fostering innovation.

In conclusion, acknowledging contributions and giving credit where it is due is not only a matter of fairness but also an investment in a motivated ecosystem that thrives on collaboration and innovation. Examples from science and technology highlight the transformative impact of recognizing the contributions of all individuals, even those who may not be immediately evident. By fostering a culture of generous recognition, we create an environment where individuals are motivated to contribute their best, knowing that their efforts will be valued and celebrated. In doing so, we not only advance knowledge and technology but also pave the way for a brighter and more inclusive future where innovation and collaboration know no bounds.

30

Unearthing Bias

The Imperative of Proactive Recognition and Growth

PSTO-30: We must try proactively to identify or recognise any bias we may have. Most of the times, we treat it as natural. That's nothing but dangerous. It's incumbent on us to work on it immediately.

Bias, whether conscious or unconscious, is a pervasive aspect of human cognition. Yet, it is our responsibility to proactively identify and recognize these biases, as ignoring them can perpetuate inequality and injustice. This chapter explores the critical notion that we must actively work to uncover and address bias within ourselves. There are numerous examples in life which highlight the importance of this endeavour and its transformative potential in fostering a more equitable and inclusive society.

1. The Challenge of Implicit Bias

Implicit bias, often hidden beneath the surface of our consciousness, can shape our attitudes and behaviours. The Implicit Association Test (IAT) developed by psychologists provides insights into our implicit biases. For example, studies using the IAT have revealed that even individuals who consciously hold egalitarian beliefs may still exhibit implicit biases related to race, gender, or other factors.

2. Unconscious Bias in the Workplace

Unconscious bias can have profound effects in the workplace. Tech giant Google conducted an internal study to examine unconscious bias in its hiring and promotion processes. The findings revealed the need for proactive efforts to counteract bias, leading to initiatives such as inclusive training and education to promote equitable opportunities for all employees. Unconscious bias in the workplace is an insidious challenge that can influence decisions, often unintentionally. For instance, during the hiring process, a manager might unconsciously favour a candidate who shares similar hobbies or background, overlooking more qualified candidates. These biases, which can be based on factors such as race, gender, or even personal affinities, can hinder diversity and inclusion, limiting opportunities for talented individuals. Recognizing and addressing unconscious bias is crucial for creating fair and equitable workplaces where everyone has an equal chance to thrive, based on their skills and potential, rather than hidden prejudices.

3. Addressing Gender Bias

Gender bias persists in various aspects of society, including leadership roles. Sheryl Sandberg, Facebook's COO, highlighted the issue of gender bias. Through her book "Lean In" and the launch of the "Lean In" movement, she has brought attention to the challenges women face in professional settings. Sandberg emphasizes the importance of women leaning into their ambitions, asserting themselves, and challenging stereotypes that perpetuate gender bias. Her leadership has encouraged open dialogues and prompted organizations to implement policies that promote gender equality, paving the way for women to break through barriers and reach their full potential in the corporate world. She urged women to recognize and confront their own biases as well as advocate for gender equality. Sandberg's call to action emphasizes the importance of proactive recognition and change.

4. Bias in Criminal Justice

Bias can also have profound consequences in the criminal justice system. The documentary film "13th" directed by Ava DuVernay explores racial bias and inequality in the U.S. prison system. The film's examination of systemic bias underscores the need for proactive efforts to address injustice and inequality.

In conclusion, recognizing and addressing bias, whether explicit or implicit, is not merely a personal endeavour but a collective responsibility. Examples from psychology, the workplace, gender equality, and criminal justice demonstrate the far-reaching impact of bias and the importance of proactive recognition and change. By acknowledging our biases and actively working to dismantle them, we contribute to a more just, equitable, and inclusive society. It is only through our collective commitment to growth and self-awareness that we can create a world where bias holds less sway, and where equality and justice flourish.

31

The Power of Challenge

Embracing Growth and Exploration

PSTO-31: We must keep challenging ourselves. This would not only help in keeping ourselves abreast with realities, it would also help us opening up new frontiers from time to time.

In the journey of personal and professional development, one constant driver of progress is the act of challenging ourselves. This chapter explores the idea that embracing challenges not only keeps us attuned to the ever-changing realities of life but also opens new frontiers of growth and exploration. Some instances from the world of sports and other fields, may resonate with the transformative power of this mindset.

1. Continual Learning and Adaptation

Challenging ourselves is a cornerstone of continual learning and adaptation. Consider the example of Sir David Attenborough, the celebrated naturalist and broadcaster. Throughout his career, Attenborough challenged himself to explore and understand the natural world. His commitment to learning has led to groundbreaking documentaries that have educated and inspired millions about the wonders of the planet.

2. Athlete's Pursuit of Excellence

Sports provide numerous examples of individuals who consistently challenge themselves to achieve excellence. Michael Jordan, widely regarded as one of the greatest basketball players of all time, continually pushed his own limits and embraced challenges. His pursuit of excellence and willingness to face adversity fuelled his success and inspired future generations of athletes.

3. Challenging the limits

Challenging the limits is exemplified by Neeraj Chopra, the Indian javelin thrower and Olympic gold medallist. Despite limited access to resources and facilities for his sport in India, Neeraj demonstrated unparalleled dedication. He broke the barriers of tradition and expectations, setting a world junior record for javelin and, eventually, winning gold at the Tokyo Olympics. Neeraj's story underlines how relentless pursuit of excellence and breaking through the constraints of one's circumstances can result in achieving unprecedented heights and rewriting what is possible, inspiring a generation of aspiring athletes and proving that potential knows no bounds.

4. Power of Challenging Self

Baba Ramdev's journey illustrates the power of self-challenge and growth. Starting as a yoga guru, he consistently pushed himself beyond traditional boundaries, venturing into health, wellness, and FMCG industries. By challenging himself to adapt to evolving realities, he not only stayed relevant but also opened up new frontiers, creating a vast business empire. His example shows how self-improvement drives both personal and professional transformation.

In conclusion, the act of challenging ourselves is a catalyst for growth, innovation, and exploration. Real-life examples from the realms of education, sports, entrepreneurship, personal growth, and exploration demonstrate the transformative power of embracing challenges. By continually pushing our own boundaries, we not only stay attuned to the ever-changing realities of life but also pave the way for new frontiers of discovery and personal achievement. It is through this willingness to challenge ourselves that we embark on journeys of self-discovery and contribute to the progress and betterment of society, as a whole.

32

The Endless Odyssey of Learning

Navigating New Avenues for Lifelong Growth

PSTO-32: Learning is a lifelong affair. The day one stops learning, she/he stops growing. It is, therefore, incumbent on us to look for newer avenues of learning.

Learning is a lifelong affair, a continuous journey that propels personal growth and evolution. It is a fundamental truth that the moment one ceases to learn, one ceases to grow. Throughout our lives, we must remain steadfast in our pursuit of knowledge, for this commitment fuels our intellectual, emotional, and personal development. Learning is a lifelong voyage, an odyssey that doesn't cease with age or circumstance. This chapter embarks on a journey through the idea that continuous learning is not just a choice but a necessity for personal growth and evolution with examples, that may illuminate the transformative power of seeking new avenues of learning throughout one's life.

1. Curiosity Beyond

Kobe Bryant, known for his legendary basketball career, was also a lifelong learner. After retiring, he delved into new fields such as storytelling, film production, and venture capital. His curiosity pushed him to continue growing even after leaving the sport, proving that learning never stops, no matter how successful one becomes. His transition from the court to the creative and business worlds is a testament to the importance of always seeking new knowledge.

2. Lifelong Learning in the Digital Age

The digital age has democratized access to learning resources. The concept of lifelong learning in digital age finds a potent example in Khan Academy, a revolutionary online education platform. Founded by Salman Khan, Khan Academy offers free, high-quality educational resources to learners of all ages. It illustrates that learning isn't confined to classrooms or specific stages of life; it's a perpetual journey. With a vast library of video lessons, exercises, and a commitment to equitable access, Khan Academy empowers individuals worldwide to acquire new skills and knowledge, from elementary subjects to advanced topics. This platform embodies the essence of lifelong learning, making education a dynamic and inclusive part of daily life for millions.

3. The Unceasing Quest for Personal Growth

Learning signifies a lifelong journey, an unceasing quest for personal growth and development. It involves constantly navigating new avenues of knowledge and experience. Take, for instance, the late Stephen Hawking, the renowned theoretical physicist. Despite facing the formidable challenges of a debilitating illness, he continued his exploration of the cosmos, authoring groundbreaking books and revolutionizing our understanding of the universe. His unwavering commitment to learning and discovery exemplifies the boundless nature of the human spirit when it embraces lifelong growth, proving that the voyage of knowledge is limitless and can transcend any obstacle.

4. The Relentless Pursuit of Expertise

Temple Grandin, a prominent autism advocate and professor of animal science, embodies the concept of the endless odyssey of learning. Despite facing the challenges of autism, she dedicated her life to understanding animal behaviour and improving their welfare in agriculture. Her pioneering work in animal husbandry and her lifelong pursuit of knowledge led to the development of more humane livestock handling systems. Grandin's journey illustrates that the path to lifelong growth can be shaped by a relentless pursuit of expertise and a commitment to making a meaningful impact, regardless of personal obstacles.

In conclusion, the pursuit of new avenues for learning is a lifelong commitment that fuels personal growth and evolution. Examples from curiosity beyond, online education, literature, life experiences, and science illustrate the transformative power of seeking knowledge throughout one's life. By embracing learning as an ongoing journey, individuals not only expand their horizons but also contribute to the betterment of society and the world. It is through the continuous exploration of new avenues that we remain adaptable, open-minded, and prepared to face the ever-evolving challenges and opportunities that life presents.

33

Embracing Diverse Perspectives

The Power of Respectful Discourse

PSTO-33: Everyone has her/his way of looking at things. But we must learn to respect everyone's views, irrespective of however contrary it may be to ours. They give us the opportunity of having newer perspectives.

In a world rich with diversity, every individual brings their unique perspective and worldview to the table. This chapter delves into the importance of respecting and valuing these varied viewpoints, even when they starkly differ from our own. We have examples that can illuminate the transformative power of embracing diverse perspectives as a means of fostering understanding and growth.

1. The Value of Constructive Debate

Respecting diverse perspectives is not about blindly agreeing but engaging in constructive debate. The founding fathers of the United States, while drafting the Constitution, had divergent views on governance. However, they engaged in spirited debates, ultimately leading to a document that has endured for centuries.

2. Scientific Progress Through Diverse Ideas

The scientific community thrives on diverse perspectives. Albert Einstein, known for his groundbreaking theories, faced opposition and skepticism from his contemporaries. However, through respectful discourse and rigorous examination, his ideas eventually revolutionized our understanding of the universe.

3. Dialogues between Perpetrators & Survivors

Desmond Tutu, the South African Anglican bishop and social rights activist, embodies the power of embracing diverse perspectives and respectful discourse. During the challenging era of apartheid, Tutu championed nonviolent resistance and reconciliation. He led the Truth and Reconciliation Commission, where survivors and perpetrators of violence engaged in open, congenial dialogue to heal the wounds of the past. Tutu's commitment to listening to diverse voices and facilitating conversations contributed to South Africa's peaceful transition to democracy. His example highlights how embracing differing viewpoints and respectful discourse can be transformative in resolving conflicts and fostering unity in divided societies.

4. The Role of Diplomacy in International Relations

In international diplomacy, respecting diverse perspectives is paramount. The Camp David Accords, facilitated by U.S. President Jimmy Carter, brought together Egyptian President Anwar Sadat and Israeli Prime Minister Menachem Begin. Despite deeply entrenched differences, they engaged in respectful dialogue, resulting in a historic peace treaty.

In conclusion, embracing diverse perspectives is a fundamental aspect of creating a more harmonious and innovative world. Real-life examples from constitutional debates, scientific progress, innovation, diplomacy, and education illustrate the transformative potential of respectful discourse. By valuing and engaging with views that differ from our own, we not only gain a deeper understanding of complex issues but also contribute to more inclusive and empathetic societies. It is through the interplay of diverse perspectives that we uncover new solutions, foster unity, and progress toward a brighter future for all.

34

The Unshakeable Spirit

Triumphing Through Faith and Resilience

PSTO-34: There would be many occasions in life, when our faith, our confidence may waver. But real fighters, and thus true winners are they, who don't get shaken up by these. Rather, they do come out stronger.

Life is an unpredictable journey, often filled with moments that test our faith and confidence. This essay delves into the idea that true winners and real fighters are those who, in the face of adversity, do not waver but emerge even stronger through unwavering faith and resilience. Real-life examples will illustrate the transformative power of maintaining a steadfast spirit.

1. Triumph Over Distress

Louis Zamperini was an American World War II veteran and former Olympic distance runner. After surviving a plane crash in the Pacific Ocean, he spent 47 days adrift on a life raft before being captured by the Japanese Navy. Zamperini endured brutal treatment as a prisoner of war for over two years. His faith in God and determination to survive helped him withstand unimaginable physical and emotional challenges. After the war, Zamperini forgave his captors and became an inspirational speaker, emphasizing the power of resilience and forgiveness.

2. Overcoming Personal Loss

Loss and grief can shake the strongest of faith, yet some individuals emerge from such experiences with greater resilience. Michelle Obama, former First Lady of the United States, endured personal losses during her childhood and later faced public scrutiny. However, her unwavering faith in the power of education and her commitment to advocating for it have left a lasting impact.

3. Overcoming Disability

Born without arms and legs, Nick Vujicic faced numerous physical and emotional challenges throughout his life. Despite the adversity, he triumphed through his faith and resilience. Nick became a motivational speaker, author, and evangelist, inspiring millions of people around the world with his story of overcoming obstacles and finding purpose.

4. Facing the Adversity Head on

Bethany Hamilton, a professional surfer, lost her left arm in a shark attack when she was just 13 years old. Instead of giving up her passion for surfing, Bethany displayed incredible resilience and faith. She returned to competitive surfing and became an inspiration for many, proving that determination can overcome even the most daunting setbacks.

5. The Perseverance of Sumit Agarwal

Born in seven months, born with cerebral palsy with 70% body restriction, Sumit's parents were not sure if he would survive. He did survive, but with severe disability. They had to see Sumit going through multiple surgeries. Samit has fought on. Today he is a TedX speaker, a youth icon on disability, speaks in conferences, advises companies on DEI and so on.

In conclusion, unwavering faith and resilience in the face of adversity define true winners and real fighters. Real-life examples from science, public service, literature, and advocacy illustrate the transformative power of maintaining a steadfast spirit. By embracing challenges as opportunities for growth, by viewing failures as stepping stones, and by holding onto their faith and convictions, individuals not only triumph over adversity but also inspire others to do the same. It is through the unshakeable spirit of such individuals that we learn the true meaning of resilience and the potential for triumph in the face of life's most formidable challenges.

35

Breaking Free

Embracing Limitless Potential Through Uninhibited Living

PSTO-35: The day we learn to let go our inhibitions completely, sky becomes the limit. Sooner we do it, better it is for us.

The idea that transcending inhibitions can unleash boundless potential forms the core of this essay. It explores the transformative power of shedding self-imposed limitations and embracing life without reservations. Real-life and cinematic examples, including those from Indian and Hollywood films, will illustrate the profound impact of letting go of inhibitions.

1. The Inspiring Tale of "Slumdog Millionaire"

The film "Slumdog Millionaire" tells the story of Jamal Malik, a young man from the slums of Mumbai, who participates in the Indian version of "Who Wants to Be a Millionaire." Jamal's journey is marked by unwavering determination and the willingness to shed inhibitions about his background and social status. By embracing each question with confidence and without hesitation, he transcends his limitations and astonishes the world.

2. "Dead Poets Society": Carpe Diem and Seize the Day

The film "Dead Poets Society" starring Robin Williams as John Keating, an English teacher, encourages his students to seize the day and pursue their passions. Keating's unorthodox teaching methods inspire his students to break free from societal expectations and follow their hearts. The film beautifully illustrates the idea that when we let go of inhibitions, we can tap into our full potential.

3. "Queen": A Journey of Self-Discovery

The Indian film "Queen" follows the story of Rani, a young woman who embarks on a solo honeymoon trip to Europe after her wedding is called off. During her journey, Rani gradually sheds her inhibitions and learns to embrace life fully. The film showcases the liberating effect of letting go of societal norms and expectations.

4. "Rocketman": Elton John's Fearless Expression

The biographical film "Rocketman" explores the life of Elton John, the iconic musician. Throughout his career, Elton John embraced flamboyant fashion and unapologetically expressed his true self. His willingness to shed inhibitions and be authentically himself not only shaped his music but also inspired countless individuals to do the same.

5. "Eat Pray Love": A Quest for Self-Discovery

In the film adaptation of the memoir "Eat Pray Love," the protagonist, Elizabeth Gilbert, embarks on a journey of self-discovery and personal growth. By shedding inhibitions and exploring different aspects of life, she finds her true self and inner peace.

In conclusion, the act of letting go of inhibitions is a profound step toward unlocking one's limitless potential. Real-life and cinematic examples from "Slumdog Millionaire," "Dead Poets

Society," "Queen," "Rocketman," and "Eat Pray Love" highlight the transformative power of embracing life without reservations. By doing so, individuals not only break free from self-imposed limitations but also inspire others to live authentically and fearlessly. It is through this courageous pursuit of life's boundless possibilities that we can reach new heights and discover the richness of our own potential.

36

Making a Difference

The Ripple Effect of Acts of Kindness

PSTO-36: We must always strive to make a difference, even if it's just in one life only. For us, it may be mundane, but for the beneficiary, it could be life-changing.

The notion that every effort to make a difference, no matter how small, can be life-changing for someone else forms the central theme of this essay. It explores the profound impact of acts of kindness and the ripple effect they create. Real-life examples will illustrate how seemingly mundane actions can have life-altering consequences for those on the receiving end.

1. The Story of Greg Mortenson's "Three Cups of Tea"

Greg Mortenson's journey to make a difference began with a simple act of thoughtfulness. Lost and disoriented in a remote Pakistani village, he was taken in by the local residents. In gratitude, Mortenson pledged to build a school for their children. This commitment evolved into a mission to promote education in remote areas, leading to the establishment of numerous schools through his Central Asia Institute.

2. Fighting Child Hunger

Marcus Rashford's campaign to end child hunger in the UK has made a difference in countless lives. What started as a personal initiative turned into a nationwide movement, as Rashford's persistence in calling for government action changed the lives of many underprivileged children, showing how even a single act of compassion can have a significant, life-changing impact.

3. The Butterfly Effect: Small Actions, Big Consequences

The butterfly effect, a concept from chaos theory, illustrates how small actions can lead to significant consequences. A smile, a kind word, or a helping hand can have a profound impact on someone's day and, in turn, influence their decisions and actions.

4. The Acts of Generosity in "Schindler's List"

The film "Schindler's List" tells the true story of Oskar Schindler, a German businessman who saved the lives of over a thousand Polish-Jewish refugees during the Holocaust. His seemingly mundane decision to employ these refugees in his factory made a life-changing difference for each one and is a testament to the power of individual actions.

In conclusion, the idea that small acts of kindness and efforts to make a difference can be life-changing for others underscores the profound impact of human compassion and generosity. Real-life and cinematic examples from Greg Mortenson's mission, fighting child hunger by Mashford, the butterfly effect, and Oskar Schindler's actions demonstrate the ripple effect of kindness. By striving to make a positive difference, even in just one life, we not only enhance the well-being of others but also contribute to a more compassionate and interconnected world. It is through these collective acts of kindness that we can create a legacy of positive change that resonates far beyond our individual actions.

37

Finding Perspective

Navigating Partings with Grace and Understanding

PSTO-37: It certainly hurts deeply when someone you always supported or vouched for, part ways on your rainy day. But we need to appreciate the context. That would certainly help us see the brighter side.

This chapter delves into the profound emotions that arise when someone we've always supported or vouched for chooses to part ways during our rainy days. It emphasizes the importance of appreciating the context surrounding such decisions and how this perspective can help us find the brighter side even amidst the hurt. Real-life examples will illustrate the transformative power of understanding and grace in times of parting.

1. The Tale of Business Ventures

Partnerships and business collaborations often face challenges, and sometimes they lead to partings. The story of Steve Jobs and John Sculley at Apple serves as an example. Despite their eventual parting, both individuals acknowledged the context and complexities that led to their separation. Steve Jobs later returned to Apple, and the company's subsequent success demonstrated the value of understanding and reconciliation.

2. Friendships That Evolve

Friendships can undergo changes, and individuals may drift apart for various reasons. Oprah Winfrey and Gayle King, renowned friends and media personalities, have experienced ups and downs in their friendship. They openly discussed their challenges, demonstrating how understanding and communication can lead to a stronger bond.

3. Overcoming Professional Criticism

In the world of sports, player transfers and coaching changes are common occurrences. The decision of a beloved player or coach to leave a team can be Cristiano Ronaldo faced intense criticism and scrutiny during his early career, especially when he left Manchester United for Real Madrid. Many fans felt betrayed and questioned his loyalty. Instead of allowing this to affect him negatively, Ronaldo used it as motivation, focusing on his performance and dedication to the game. His success at Real Madrid turned the criticism into admiration, showcasing his ability to appreciate the broader context and thrive despite adversity.

4. Political Alliances and Partings

In the realm of politics, alliances can shift due to differing ideologies or changing circumstances. The example of Winston Churchill and Joseph Stalin during World War II illustrates how wartime alliances can evolve. Understanding the geopolitical context at the time sheds light on the complex decisions made during those tumultuous years.

5. The Arc of Personal Relationships

Personal relationships often face trials and tribulations. The enduring friendship between Mahatma Gandhi and Hermann

Kallenbach provides insights into the complexities of human relationships. Despite challenges and temporary partings, their bond remained strong, emphasizing the value of understanding and forgiveness.

In conclusion, partings with those we've supported or vouched for can be emotionally challenging, but finding perspective is essential for personal growth and reconciliation. Real-life examples from business ventures, friendships, sports, politics, and personal relationships demonstrate the transformative power of understanding and grace. By appreciating the context and complexities that surround such decisions, we not only find the brighter side but also pave the way for potential reconciliation and personal growth. It is through these acts of understanding that we foster empathy, forgiveness, and resilience in the face of life's inevitable transitions.

38

The Triad of Success

Patience, Perseverance, and Diligence

PSTO-38: Patience and Perseverance are very important to be successful in life. But Diligence is equally important. It bridges the gap between Aspirations and Current Status.

This essay explores the symbiotic relationship between patience, perseverance, and diligence in the journey to success. It emphasizes that while patience and perseverance are critical, it is diligence that acts as the bridge between one's aspirations and their current status. Real-life examples will illustrate how this triad can lead to remarkable achievements.

1. Consistent Excellence

Tom Brady, widely regarded as one of the greatest quarterbacks in NFL history, exemplifies patience, perseverance, and diligence. Despite being drafted in the sixth round of the NFL Draft, he worked tirelessly to improve his skills, leading to multiple Super Bowl victories. Brady's disciplined approach to training, preparation, and execution highlights how diligence bridges the gap between aspiration and achievement, inspiring athletes worldwide to strive for greatness through hard work.

2. The Marathon of Endurance

Endurance sports like marathons exemplify the importance of patience, perseverance, and diligence. Eliud Kipchoge, the Kenyan long-distance runner, patiently honed his skills, persevered through countless hours of training, and displayed unwavering diligence in perfecting his craft. His remarkable feat of breaking the two-hour marathon barrier showcased the triumphant synergy of these qualities.

3. The Grit

Angela Duckworth, in her research and book "Grit: The Power of Passion and Perseverance," emphasizes the importance of perseverance and diligence in achieving long-term goals. Through her studies, Duckworth found that grit, a combination of passion and perseverance, plays a significant role in determining success. Individuals who consistently apply effort and remain dedicated to their objectives, even in the face of challenges, are more likely to achieve success over time.

4. The Diligence, personified

Sara Blakely is the founder of Spanx, a billion-dollar hosiery company. When she started, Blakely faced multiple challenges, including lack of industry experience and rejection from potential investors. Despite the setbacks, she remained persistent, patiently refining her product and persevering through the initial hurdles of entrepreneurship. Blakely's diligence in building her business from the ground up ultimately led to the success of Spanx.

5. Perseverance pays

Temie Giwa-Tubosun is a Nigerian-American entrepreneur and

the founder of LifeBank, a medical distribution company focused on improving access to blood transfusions and medical products in Nigeria. Giwa-Tubosun faced numerous challenges in establishing LifeBank, including logistical hurdles and cultural barriers related to blood donation. Despite the obstacles, she exhibited patience, perseverance, and diligence in addressing the critical issue of blood shortages in Nigeria's healthcare system.

Giwa-Tubosun's commitment to her mission led to the development of innovative solutions, such as using technology to match blood donors with hospitals in need. Her patient and persistent efforts have not only saved lives but have also garnered international recognition for the impact of LifeBank. Giwa-Tubosun's journey exemplifies how a combination of patience, perseverance, and diligence can drive positive change and success in addressing pressing societal issues.

In conclusion, success is often built on the foundation of patience, perseverance, and diligence. Real-life examples from inventors, athletes, artists, tech visionaries, and advocates demonstrate the transformative power of this triad. While patience allows us to weather challenges, perseverance keeps us moving forward, and diligence bridges the gap between our aspirations and current status. It is through the harmonious interplay of these qualities that we can achieve remarkable feats and leave a lasting legacy of achievement in our chosen endeavors.

39

Nature's Embrace

Finding Solace and Inspiration in the Natural World

PSTO-39: Nature is so beautiful. It not only calms you, it also inspires you to get going. Spending a few minutes in the lap of nature is a big blessing.

This chapter celebrates the profound beauty and therapeutic power of nature. It explores how nature has the ability not only to soothe and calm but also to inspire and rejuvenate the human spirit. Real-life examples will illustrate the transformative impact of spending time in the embrace of the natural world.

1. The Healing Power of Forest Bathing

Shinrin-yoku, or forest bathing, is a Japanese practice that involves immersing oneself in the sights, sounds, and scents of a forest. Research has shown that spending time in a forest environment can reduce stress, lower blood pressure, and boost mood. This practice demonstrates how nature can provide a sanctuary of calm and healing.

2. Thoreau's Walden Pond

Henry David Thoreau, the American transcendentalist, famously spent two years living in a cabin by Walden Pond. His experiences in nature inspired his writings on simplicity, self-reliance, and the beauty of the natural world. Thoreau's reflections on the tranquility and inspiration found in nature continue to resonate with readers today.

3. The Eco-Warrior from Rajasthan

Baba Budhmal, a humble farmer from Rajasthan, found inspiration and calm in nature, particularly in trees. Over decades, he planted and nurtured thousands of trees in the barren lands of Rajasthan. His belief that nature can heal and inspire led him to transform the landscape, not only for his personal fulfilment but also for the benefit of future generations.

4. Nature's Role in Mental Health

Studies have shown that spending time in natural settings can have a positive impact on mental health. The Mindful Attention Awareness Scale (MAAS) measures an individual's ability to be fully present and engage with their surroundings. Research has found that people who spend more time in natural environments tend to score higher on the MAAS, indicating greater mindfulness and emotional well-being.

5. The Inspiration from Nature

Valmik Thapar, a leading wildlife conservationist in India, draws inspiration from nature, especially the majestic tigers of India. Spending extensive time in forests, he was inspired to dedicate his life to preserving India's wildlife. His deep connection with nature not only brought him peace but also motivated him to spearhead several wildlife conservation efforts across the country.

In conclusion, the beauty of nature is a source of solace and inspiration that has the capacity to heal and rejuvenate the human spirit. Real-life examples from practices like forest bathing, the writings of Thoreau, eco-warrior Baba Budhamal, research on nature's impact on mental health, and efforts of Valmik Thapar illustrate the transformative power of spending time in nature's embrace. Whether it's a walk in the woods, a visit to a national park, or simply gazing at a starry night sky, nature provides a profound blessing that can calm the soul and ignite the spark of inspiration within us.

40

Embracing Life's Lessons

The Value of Every Encounter

PSTO-40: Every person you meet in the journey of life, has something to offer you. It can always add a fresh page in our lessons of life. It is incumbent on us to sense it and grab it.

This chapter delves into the idea that every person we encounter on the journey of life has something valuable to offer us. It emphasizes the importance of remaining open and receptive to the lessons and insights that each interaction can provide. Real-life examples will illustrate how seizing these opportunities can lead to personal growth and enriched life experiences.

1. The Wisdom of People around You

Ratan Tata, during his tenure as the chairman of Tata Sons, demonstrated the belief that every person he encountered had something valuable to offer. Under his leadership, the Tata Group expanded globally and diversified into various industries. One notable instance was the acquisition of Jaguar Land Rover. Despite being a significant move, Tata sought to learn from the existing talent within the acquired company rather than imposing immediate changes. His approach reflected a deep understanding that the individuals he met in the journey of business had unique insights and experiences to contribute. Ratan Tata's ability to sense and value the potential contributions of people from diverse backgrounds and industries allowed him to navigate complex business scenarios successfully.

2. Learning from Child Labourers

Kailash Satyarthi, the Nobel Peace Prize laureate, has dedicated his life to fighting child labor. Through his encounters with child laborers, he learned about the devastating effects of exploitation and the resilience of children. Each child he rescued offered him insights into the complexities of human suffering, giving him a deeper understanding of what it takes to mobilize global movements for change.

3. Learning from Farmers

Dr. M.S. Swaminathan, known as the father of India's Green Revolution, spent significant time interacting with farmers in remote regions. He learned about their indigenous farming practices, environmental challenges, and the impact of monsoons on crop yields. The insights he gained from these interactions were instrumental in shaping his approach to developing high-yielding varieties of crops, which revolutionized Indian agriculture.

4. Journey from Tea-seller to Author

Laxman Rao is a tea seller in Delhi who has authored over 25 books. His inspiration came from the customers he served tea to. Conversations with everyday people provided him with material for his stories, each interaction adding a new dimension to his understanding of society. His belief in learning from everyone around him enabled him to become a successful self-published author, despite his humble background.

5. The Impact of Mentors

Narayana Murthy, as the co-founder of Infosys, emphasized the importance of learning from every person encountered in the professional journey. In the early days of Infosys, Murthy and his team faced challenges in the competitive IT industry. Murthy recognized the significance of surrounding himself with talented individuals and learning from their expertise.

Throughout his career, Murthy has been known for seeking advice and guidance from various professionals, including those younger or less experienced. This openness to learning from others, regardless of their position or background, has played a crucial role in Infosys's success and Murthy's reputation as a visionary leader in the technology sector.

In conclusion, the people we encounter on our life journey—whether elders, peers, strangers, those from different cultures, or mentors—all have something to offer us. Real-life examples from Ratan Tata, Kailash Satyarthi, M. S. Swaminathan, Laxman Rao and Narayana Murthy demonstrate the transformative power of these encounters. By remaining open to the lessons and wisdom that others can impart, we not only enrich our own understanding but also create opportunities for personal growth, empathy, and a deeper appreciation for the diversity of human experiences. It is through these interactions that we add fresh pages to our life's lessons, contributing to a more enriched and enlightened existence.

41

Unleashing the Power of Time

A Journey Through Time and Motion

PSTO-41: How often do we complain that we don't have time? But, have we tried a time & motion study of our daily activities? If we do, we probably would end up with so much of surplus time!! So it's time to plan our daily chores really well

This chapter explores the common lament of not having enough time and suggests that a time and motion study of our daily activities can reveal hidden pockets of surplus time. It underscores the importance of meticulously planning our daily chores to optimize our time management. Real-life examples will illustrate how such an approach can lead to a more productive and balanced life.

1. The Story of Benjamin Franklin

Benjamin Franklin, one of the Founding Fathers of the United States, was a master of time management. He famously created a daily schedule that allocated specific time blocks for various activities, from work to leisure and self-improvement. Franklin's commitment to structured planning enabled him to achieve remarkable productivity and make significant contributions to society.

2. Time-tracking Apps and Tools

In today's digital age, various time-tracking apps and tools are available to help individuals gain insights into how they spend their time. Apps like Toggl and RescueTime allow users to monitor their daily activities, revealing patterns and areas where time could be better managed.

3. The Impact of the Pomodoro Technique

The Pomodoro Technique, developed by Francesco Cirillo, is a time management method that involves working in focused intervals (typically 25 minutes) followed by short breaks. This technique has been widely adopted by professionals and students alike to enhance productivity by efficiently utilizing time.

4. The Benefits of Prioritization

Effective time management involves prioritizing tasks based on importance and urgency. Dwight D. Eisenhower, the 34th President of the United States, devised the Eisenhower Matrix, a tool for categorizing tasks into four quadrants: urgent and important, not urgent but important, urgent but not important, and neither urgent nor important. This matrix aids in making informed decisions about how to allocate time and effort.

5. Time Management in Creative Pursuits

Even in creative fields, time management is essential. Renowned author Stephen King, known for his prolific output, emphasizes the importance of setting specific writing goals and adhering to a regular writing schedule. His commitment to disciplined writing practices has enabled him to produce numerous bestsellers.

In conclusion, the complaint of not having enough time can often be addressed through meticulous planning and effective time management. Real-life examples from Benjamin Franklin's structured daily schedule, modern time-tracking tools, the Pomodoro Technique, the Eisenhower Matrix, and Stephen King's writing discipline demonstrate the transformative power of optimizing time management. By conducting a time and motion study of our daily activities and strategically planning our chores, we can unlock hidden reserves of surplus time. This surplus time can then be reinvested in personal growth, relaxation, or pursuing meaningful endeavors, ultimately leading to a more balanced and fulfilling life.

42

The Art of Mindfulness

Anchoring Our Thoughts to the Present

PSTO-42: Many a time, we are there, but still we are not, with our mind wavering away from present! We must consciously try to rein it.

This chapter delves into the common experience of being physically present but mentally absent, and it emphasizes the importance of practicing mindfulness to consciously anchor our thoughts to the present moment. Real-life examples will illustrate how mindfulness can enhance our focus, well-being, and overall quality of life.

1. Overcoming Mental Challenges

Simone Biles, the world-renowned gymnast, has spoken about the struggles of keeping her mind present in the face of pressure and mental health challenges. During the 2020 Tokyo Olympics, she chose to step back from competition to focus on her mental well-being. By consciously recognizing when her mind was not in the present moment, Biles exemplified the importance of mental clarity, showing that it takes conscious effort to stay focused.

2. The Power of Breath Awareness

One fundamental aspect of mindfulness is breath awareness. By paying attention to our breath and the sensations it generates, we can bring our wandering minds back to the present moment. The "4-7-8" breathing technique, developed by Dr. Andrew Weil, is a simple yet effective way to anchor the mind to the present and induce relaxation.

3. The Impact on Mental Health

Studies have shown that practicing mindfulness can have a significant impact on mental health. Jon Kabat-Zinn's Mindfulness-Based Stress Reduction (MBSR) program, for example, has helped individuals cope with anxiety, depression, and chronic pain by cultivating mindfulness. This approach highlights the potential of mindfulness to enhance emotional well-being.

4. The Zen of Everyday Activities

Mindfulness need not be limited to formal meditation. Everyday activities like washing dishes, gardening, or taking a walk can become opportunities for mindfulness. Thich Nhat Hanh, a Zen master, encourages individuals to approach such activities with full presence and attention, transforming them into meditative practices.

5. Workplace Mindfulness Practice

During a busy workday, we find ourselves multitasking and juggling various responsibilities. While physically present at our desk, our mind may wander to future projects, worries, or unrelated thoughts. Realizing the importance of being present and focused, we must decide to practice mindfulness at work. We must take short breaks to engage in mindful breathing, bringing our attention back to the current task at hand. This conscious effort to rein in our wandering mind enhances productivity and the quality of our work.

In conclusion, the phenomenon of being physically present but mentally absent is a common challenge in today's fast-paced world. Real-life examples from breath awareness techniques, mental health interventions like MBSR, the Zen approach to everyday activities, workplace mindfulness practice demonstrate the transformative power of mindfulness. By consciously practicing mindfulness and anchoring our thoughts to the present moment, we can enhance our focus, emotional well-being, and overall quality of life. It is through this practice that we can fully experience the richness and beauty of each moment, leading to a more fulfilling and mindful existence.

43

Beyond the Clock

The Universal Virtue of Punctuality

PSTO-43: Punctuality is a virtue that every human being must possess. But it's not limited to arrival or attendance times only. It must be displayed during every facet of our activities.

This essay explores the concept of punctuality as a virtue that extends beyond simply arriving or attending on time. It emphasizes that punctuality should be displayed in every facet of our activities, from keeping promises to meeting deadlines. Real-life examples will illustrate how practicing punctuality can lead to personal and professional success.

1. The Precision of Swiss Watches

Switzerland is renowned for its precision in watchmaking. Swiss watchmakers are not only punctual in the sense of producing timepieces that keep accurate time, but they also reflect the cultural value of punctuality in their work ethic. The reputation of Swiss watches exemplifies how punctuality is a cornerstone of excellence.

2. Leading by Example

Indra Nooyi, the former CEO of PepsiCo, is known for her punctuality in the business world. She often emphasized the value of time management and adhering to schedules during her leadership at PepsiCo. Nooyi's commitment to punctuality in corporate settings reflects her disciplined approach to business and effective leadership. She took it beyond just office to every action or decision she took.

3. The Efficiency of Meeting Deadlines

In professional settings, meeting deadlines is a critical demonstration of punctuality. Condoleezza Rice, former U.S. Secretary of State, is recognized for her punctuality in diplomatic and political affairs. Rice has often emphasized the importance of adhering to schedules during international negotiations and meetings. Her commitment to meeting deadlines reflects a diplomatic professionalism that contributes to the success of diplomatic initiatives and fosters positive relationships on the global stage.

4. The Art of Time Management

Effective time management is an essential skill that incorporates punctuality. Tim Cook, the CEO of Apple Inc., is known for his disciplined daily routine and punctual approach to work. His dedication to managing time efficiently enables him to lead a global tech giant effectively.

5. Punctuality in Daily Life

Tom Hanks, the highly respected actor and filmmaker, is known for his punctuality on film sets. He values the time and efforts of the entire film crew, ensuring that production runs smoothly and stays on schedule. Hanks' commitment to punctuality is seen as contributing to the positive working atmosphere on set and the timely completion of film projects.

In conclusion, punctuality is a universal virtue that transcends mere timekeeping. Real-life examples from Swiss watchmakers' precision, industry leaders like Indra Nooyi, deadline-oriented leaders such as Condoleezza Rice, time management experts like Tim Cook, and punctual individuals like Tom Hanks illustrate how practicing punctuality can lead to personal and professional success. By embodying punctuality in every facet of our activities, we not only demonstrate respect for others but also create a foundation for trust, efficiency, and excellence in all that we do. It is through this commitment to punctuality that we can achieve both personal fulfilment and professional achievements.

44

The Power of Deconstruction

Breaking Down Problems for Effective Solutions

PSTO-44: Do not look at any problem as one entity. See if you can break it into smaller parts. Resolving it will be much easier.

This chapter explores the strategy of breaking down complex problems into smaller, more manageable parts and highlights how this approach simplifies the problem-solving process. Real-life examples will illustrate the transformative impact of deconstruction in various domains, from science and engineering to everyday challenges.

1. NASA's Apollo 13 Mission

The Apollo 13 mission faced a life-threatening crisis when an oxygen tank exploded in space. NASA engineers had to solve multiple interrelated problems to ensure the safe return of the astronauts. They deconstructed the overarching issue into smaller challenges, addressing each one systematically. By breaking down the problem, they successfully guided the spacecraft back to Earth.

2. Engineering Marvels

In civil engineering, the construction of large infrastructure projects often involves numerous complex components. For example, building a suspension bridge requires deconstructing the overall design into elements like cables, towers, and roadways. Engineers can then focus on solving each component's challenges, ultimately achieving the grander goal of completing the bridge.

3. Scientific Discoveries

Scientific research often involves deconstructing complex phenomena into smaller experiments or observations. For instance, in the study of genetics, researchers break down intricate genetic processes into simpler genetic pathways. This approach allows them to understand genetic mechanisms step by step, contributing to significant scientific discoveries.

4. Problem-solving in Education

In education, breaking down complex concepts into smaller, digestible units is a well-established teaching strategy. The "chunking" method, for example, helps students learn and retain information more effectively. By deconstructing a subject into manageable parts, educators enable students to grasp the material gradually.

5. Everyday Problem-solving

In daily life, individuals often face multifaceted challenges. Take moving to a new city as an example. This major life change involves various subproblems such as finding housing, securing employment, and establishing a social network. Deconstructing the relocation process into smaller tasks makes it more manageable and less overwhelming.

In conclusion, the strategy of breaking down complex problems into smaller parts is a powerful problem-solving approach that can be applied across various domains. Real-life examples, from NASA's Apollo 13 mission to everyday challenges like moving to a new city, illustrate the transformative impact of deconstruction. By dissecting problems into manageable components, we simplify the problem-solving process, enhance our understanding, and increase our chances of finding effective solutions. It is through this methodical approach that we can tackle even the most intricate problems and achieve remarkable results.

45

Lessons from the Pandemic

Self-Care as a Prerequisite for Caring for Others

PSTO-45: COVID taught us many lessons. One of the prominent ones for me has been: Please take care of yourself so that you are in a position to take care of others.

This chapter reflects on the profound lessons imparted by the COVID-19 pandemic, with a focus on the importance of self-care as a foundation for caring for others. It emphasizes how prioritizing our own well-being enables us to better support and uplift those around us. Real-life examples will illustrate the significance of this lesson in various contexts.

1. Healthcare Professionals' Sacrifice

Healthcare workers worldwide made immense sacrifices during the pandemic. Their dedication to caring for COVID-19 patients came at a personal cost, often working long hours under stressful conditions. Many healthcare professionals emphasized the importance of self-care to maintain their physical and mental health. By prioritizing their well-being, they were better equipped to provide quality care to patients.

2. The Oxygen Mask Analogy

The pre-flight safety instruction to secure your oxygen mask before assisting others is a powerful analogy for self-care. If you neglect your own oxygen needs, you won't be in a position to help fellow passengers. This principle applies to life outside of airplanes as well—ensuring your well-being is the first step in being able to support others effectively.

3. Parental Self-Care

Parents faced unique challenges during the pandemic, juggling work, childcare, and household responsibilities. Recognizing the importance of self-care, many parents took intentional breaks to recharge, knowing that their well-being directly impacted their ability to nurture and care for their children.

4. Mental Health Awareness

The pandemic spotlighted the significance of mental health. Individuals who practiced self-care by seeking therapy, engaging in mindfulness, or fostering connections with loved ones were better equipped to support family and friends facing emotional challenges.

5. Community Resilience

Communities that encouraged self-care initiatives, such as wellness check-ins and mutual aid networks, demonstrated the strength of collective well-being. These communities realized that by supporting individuals in taking care of themselves, they could foster a culture of care for others.

In conclusion, the COVID-19 pandemic has taught us a profound lesson: self-care is not selfish; it is a prerequisite for effectively caring for others. Real-life examples, from healthcare professionals to parents and communities, highlight how prioritizing our well-being empowers us to provide support, empathy, and care to those in need. By recognizing the importance of self-care and making it a cornerstone of our lives, we not only safeguard our own health and resilience but also become a source of strength and support for our communities and the world at large. It is through this balance that we can navigate challenges with compassion and resilience, emerging from adversity stronger and more united.

46

The Power of Self-Initiated Change

Becoming the 'Man in the Mirror'

PSTO-46: If you have to change yourself, it has to be driven by one person only; that is you. It is you who should determine what change you would like to see in yourself so that the 'man in the mirror' feels proud.

This essay delves into the transformative journey of self-initiated change and highlights the notion that change must be driven by one person—ourselves. It emphasizes the importance of self-determination in shaping the positive changes we aspire to see in ourselves. Real-life examples will illustrate the profound impact of self-motivated transformation.

1. Michael Jackson's "Man in the Mirror"

The iconic song "Man in the Mirror" by Michael Jackson speaks to the idea that change begins with self-reflection and self-initiated action. The lyrics convey the message that if we want to make the world a better place, we must start by changing ourselves. Jackson's personal journey of self-improvement serves as a powerful example of the transformative impact of self-initiated change.

2. Changing the face of Women's Cricket in India

Mithali Raj, captain of the Indian women cricket team, decided early in her career that she wanted to be a trailblazer in women's cricket. Facing limited recognition and opportunities, Mithali transformed herself into a world-class player, constantly pushing her own limits and setting new records. Her decision to change herself—to evolve her game and her mindset—was entirely self-driven. She set a new standard in women's cricket, ensuring that her legacy would leave the 'man in the mirror' proud of her contributions to the sport.

3. Personal Development Leaders

Leaders in the field of personal development and self-help, such as Tony Robbins and Brené Brown, advocate for self-initiated change. They emphasize that individuals have the power to change their beliefs, habits, and behaviors to create more fulfilling and purposeful lives.

4. Overcoming Ultra Bad Phases in Life

Sanjay Dutt, the renowned Bollywood actor, has had a life marked by challenges and personal struggles. Throughout his career, he faced legal issues and spent time in prison. However, he has undergone a remarkable transformation, both personally and professionally. Sanjay Dutt's journey of change was not imposed externally but was driven by his own realization of the need for transformation. He recognized the impact of his choices on his life and the lives of those around him. It was a deeply personal decision to bring about positive changes, not just for the sake of public perception but for his own sense of self and well-being.

5. From Tragedy to Triumph

Arunima Sinha, a national-level volleyball player, lost her leg in a tragic accident. Determined to make her 'man in the mirror' proud, she decided to climb Mount Everest, an audacious goal for anyone, let alone an amputee. The change she needed was completely self-driven, fueled by her desire to prove to herself that she could still achieve greatness. Her inner strength and determination made her the world's first female amputee to scale Mount Everest, showing that true change comes from within.

In conclusion, the journey of self-initiated change is a powerful and transformative one. Real-life examples, from Michael Jackson's anthem to the transformation of Sanjay Dutt, as well as stories of Mithali Raj and Arunima Sinha demonstrate the profound impact of self-motivated transformation. By recognizing that change begins within ourselves and by taking intentional steps toward self-improvement, we not only become the change we wish to see but also inspire others to embark on their own journeys of positive transformation. It is through this commitment to self-initiated change that we can create a ripple effect of growth, empowerment, and positive impact in our lives and the world around us.

47

The Art of Active Listening

Beyond Hearing Words

PSTO-47: Listening is an art. How often do we find ourselves that we are only hearing the words? 'We need to be conscious of it' ALWAYS.

This essay explores the notion that listening is indeed an art, one that goes beyond mere hearing of words. It emphasizes the importance of conscious and active listening in our interactions with others. Real-life examples will illustrate how mastering this art can lead to more meaningful connections and effective communication.

1. The Wisdom of Elders

Elders often possess a wealth of knowledge and life experiences. However, their stories and insights can be overlooked if we merely hear their words without truly listening. Taking the time to actively listen to their narratives can reveal valuable life lessons. This not only enriches our understanding but also honors their wisdom.

2. Nurturing Relationships

In personal relationships, active listening is essential for fostering understanding and empathy. Consider a couple facing a disagreement. If both partners truly listen to each other's perspectives rather than just hearing the words, they can find common ground and strengthen their bond.

3. Effective Leadership

Effective leaders are often skilled listeners. They not only hear the concerns and ideas of their team members but actively engage in meaningful dialogue. This approach fosters trust and encourages open communication, leading to more innovative solutions and a positive work environment.

4. Conflict Resolution

Active listening plays a pivotal role in resolving conflicts. Mediators and conflict resolution professionals are trained to go beyond hearing words by actively listening to the underlying emotions and needs of those involved. This skill helps them guide individuals toward peaceful resolutions.

5. Empathy and Understanding

Temple Grandin, an accomplished animal scientist and advocate for individuals with autism, provides a powerful example of the art of listening. Grandin, who is on the autism spectrum herself, has often spoken about the importance of understanding different ways of perceiving the world, particularly for those with neurodevelopmental conditions. In her advocacy work, Grandin emphasizes the significance of active listening, not just with words but with all the senses. In her role as an animal scientist, Grandin applied her unique way of perceiving the world to design more humane and efficient livestock handling systems. Her ability to "listen" to the needs and behaviours of animals, often non-verbally, allowed her to create innovative solutions that have had a significant impact on the welfare of animals in the agricultural industry.

In conclusion, the art of active listening transcends the act of hearing words. Real-life examples, from learning from elders and nurturing relationships to effective leadership and conflict resolution, highlight the transformative impact of conscious and active listening. By making a conscious effort to truly listen to others, we create opportunities for more profound connections, improved communication, and enhanced empathy. It is through this art that we can bridge gaps, build understanding, and foster a more compassionate and harmonious world.

48

Finding Fulfilment in All You Do

The Art of Loving Your Work

PSTO-48: Many of us dream to work on something that we love. But, have we ever realised that it would be equally interesting and satisfying, if we love everything that we are working on?

This essay explores the idea that finding satisfaction in your work is not solely about doing what you love; it's equally about learning to love everything you do. It emphasizes the importance of cultivating a positive mindset and finding joy in every task, regardless of its nature. Real-life examples will illustrate how this approach can lead to greater fulfilment and success.

1. Lata Mangeshkar and her Passion for Music

Lata Mangeshkar, the legendary playback singer in the Indian film industry, is an example of someone who found joy and satisfaction in every aspect of her work. While she was renowned for her soulful singing, her love for music extended beyond just performing. Mangeshkar expressed a genuine passion for every element of the music-making process, including understanding the lyrics, collaborating with composers and lyricists, and contributing to the overall artistic vision of a song. Her ability to appreciate and love every facet of her work contributed not only to her success but also to her enduring legacy in the world of music.

2. The Chef's Love for the Craft

Renowned chefs are known for their dedication to the culinary arts. They don't just love creating signature dishes; they also take pleasure in mastering the fundamentals, such as chopping, slicing, and sautéing. Their genuine love for the entire cooking process contributes to their culinary excellence.

3. Mastering Multiple Roles in Filmmaking

Satyajit Ray, the legendary filmmaker, didn't just stick to directing. He embraced multiple roles, from scriptwriting and editing to designing posters and composing music for his films. Ray found satisfaction in loving every aspect of filmmaking, even though many of these tasks were new to him when he started. His passion for all the little details of the filmmaking process helped him produce some of India's finest cinematic works, proving that loving everything you do, rather than just one part, leads to fulfilling results.

4. Everyday Joy in any Responsibility

Dr. APJ Abdul Kalam, a distinguished scientist and the 11th President of India, provides another example of someone who loved everything he worked on. Beyond his significant contributions to space and defense technology, Dr. Kalam had a profound love for education, mentorship, and inspiring young minds. Even in administrative and leadership roles, he demonstrated a genuine passion for interacting with students, encouraging innovation, and promoting the pursuit of knowledge. Dr. Kalam's enthusiasm for diverse aspects of his work, whether it was scientific research, policy formulation, or educational initiatives, made him a beloved figure in India and around the world. His example underscores the idea that finding joy and interest in every dimension of one's responsibilities can lead to a more enriching and purposeful professional journey.

In conclusion, the secret to finding fulfilment in your work lies not only in doing what you love but also in learning to love everything you do. Real-life examples, from Lata Mangeshkar's passion for music to Satyajit Ray's mastering multiple roles in filmmaking and Dr. Abdul Kalam's finding joy everywhere, demonstrate how adopting a positive and holistic mindset can lead to greater satisfaction and success. By infusing love into every aspect of our work, we not only elevate the quality of our output but also cultivate a sense of fulfilment that transcends the specific tasks we undertake. It is through this approach that we can lead more joyful and meaningful professional and personal lives.

49

Shifting Perspective

Celebrating the Innumerable Acts of Goodness

PSTO-49: It is so easy to remember someone doing some harm, however little or even perceived it may be. How many of us remember those tons of good, done by innumerable people around us?

This essay explores the human tendency to remember negative actions more readily than positive ones and emphasizes the importance of shifting our perspective to celebrate the countless acts of goodness that surround us daily. Real-life examples will illustrate how recognizing and appreciating these acts can lead to a more positive and grateful outlook.

1. The News Bias

Media often highlight negative news stories, which can skew our perception of the world. While negative events are undoubtedly important to address, they shouldn't overshadow the countless acts of kindness and goodness happening daily. Recognizing this bias is the first step in shifting our perspective.

2. Acts of Compassion

Mother Teresa, known for her selfless dedication to helping the poor and sick, provides a powerful example of someone who devoted her life to doing immense good. Despite facing numerous challenges and working in difficult conditions, she never wavered in her commitment to serving the less fortunate. Her humanitarian work in the slums of Kolkata showcased her unwavering compassion and dedication to alleviating suffering. Mother Teresa's work often involved countless small acts of compassion that might have gone unnoticed. Her focus was on the individuals she served, and her philosophy was rooted in the belief that even small acts of love and kindness could make a significant difference in the lives of others. Her life exemplifies the idea that the memory of good deeds should endure, even when overshadowed by negative perceptions or criticisms.

3. Unsung Heroes

Many people work tirelessly behind the scenes to make a positive difference in their communities. Volunteers, caregivers, and essential workers are often unsung heroes, dedicating their time and energy to help others. Their contributions deserve recognition and gratitude.

4. Generosity of Strangers

Strangers often step in to help during times of crisis. Whether it's assisting during a car breakdown or offering support during a natural disaster, these acts of goodness should be remembered and celebrated as a testament to human compassion.

5. Acts of Generosity beyond the Routine

Jamshedji Tata, the founder of the Tata Group, was not only a visionary industrialist but also a philanthropist with a deep commitment to societal welfare, who went beyond the normal call on an Industrialist. While his contributions to the business world are well-known, his efforts to improve the quality of life for communities extended beyond industrial pursuits. Tata was instrumental in establishing educational and healthcare institutions, including the Indian Institute of Science (IISc) and Tata Memorial Hospital.

In conclusion, it is common for humans to remember harm more readily than goodness. However, by consciously shifting our perspective and focusing on the innumerable acts of compassion, and generosity happening around us, we can cultivate a more positive and grateful outlook on life. Real-life examples, from random acts of kindness and unsung heroes to the generosity of strangers and going beyond the routine, demonstrate that goodness is abundant. By celebrating and acknowledging these acts, we not only uplift ourselves but also inspire a ripple effect of kindness and positivity in our communities and the world. It is through this collective recognition that we can create a more compassionate and harmonious society.

50

The Currency of Kindness

Enriching Lives, One Act at a Time

PSTO-50: One act of kindness or compassion may not cost us a fortune. Yet it may be enough to make someone fortunate. Please look for opportunity to be kind and compassionate.

This chapter explores the profound impact of acts of kindness and compassion, emphasizing that even small gestures can make a significant difference in someone's life. It encourages readers to actively seek opportunities to be kind and compassionate. Real-life examples will illustrate the transformative power of these actions.

1. The Power of a Smile

A simple smile can brighten someone's day and create a connection between strangers. Smiling at a cashier, a passerby, or a colleague can be an act of kindness that costs nothing but has the potential to uplift someone's spirit.

2. Feeding the Hungry

Donating food to a local food bank or sharing a meal with a homeless person can alleviate hunger and provide comfort to those in need. Such acts of compassion demonstrate that a single meal can make a significant difference in someone's life.

3. Acts of Listening

Actively listening to someone in distress or providing a shoulder to lean on during tough times can be incredibly compassionate. Taking the time to understand and empathize with someone's struggles can offer solace and support.

4. Mentorship and Guidance

Mentoring a young person, offering career advice, or helping someone acquire a new skill can be life-changing. The guidance and support provided through mentorship can empower individuals to reach their full potential.

5. Random Acts of Kindness

Engaging in random acts of kindness, such as leaving an encouraging note for a coworker, paying for a stranger's coffee, or helping a neighbor with chores, showcases the limitless opportunities for compassion in our daily lives.

6. Volunteering

Devoting time to volunteer for a cause you care about demonstrates a deep commitment to making a positive impact. Whether it's assisting at a local shelter, participating in community clean-ups, or volunteering at a school, these acts of kindness contribute to the betterment of society.

In conclusion, one act of kindness or compassion may not come with a hefty price tag, but its impact can be immeasurable. Real-life examples, from sharing a smile to volunteering in the community, illustrate the transformative power of these actions. By actively seeking opportunities to be kind and compassionate, we not only enrich the lives of others but also experience the profound satisfaction of knowing that our actions have made someone else's journey a little brighter. It is through these countless acts of kindness and compassion that we create a more empathetic, connected, and caring world.

51

Counting Our Blessings

The Privileges We Often Overlook

PSTO-51: Do we ever realise how privileged we are? Yet, sadly we often complain about what we do not have. We just have to look around to realise our misconception and thus remain ever thankful to Almighty for everything that we have.

In a world filled with desires and ambitions, it's easy to overlook the countless privileges we enjoy daily. Often, we become consumed by what we don't have, forgetting to appreciate what we do. This chapter explores some of the fundamental privileges we often take for granted, using real-life examples to underscore their significance.

1. Shelter: A Basic Necessity

In bustling urban streets, amid towering skyscrapers, we often encounter homeless individuals who lack the security of a home. Their existence highlights the privilege of having a place to call home, where we can seek shelter, rest, and find warmth. For many, a home is a distant dream, emphasizing the importance of valuing the roofs over our heads.

2. Education: A Path to Enlightenment

Access to education is a privilege that transforms lives. In many parts of the world, quality education is a luxury, particularly for girls. Yet, for those of us who have the opportunity to learn and grow through schooling, it's essential to recognize this privilege and make the most of it. Education empowers us to shape our futures and contribute positively to society.

3. Healthcare: The Gift of Well-being

"Health is wealth," they say, and it's a privilege we often take for granted. Many individuals face significant health challenges, sometimes without access to proper medical care. Those of us with access to healthcare facilities and the ability to address our health concerns should be grateful for this privilege. Good health allows us to pursue our dreams and live fulfilling lives.

4. Family and Friendship: A Support System

In a world where technology connects us globally, we can communicate with loved ones instantly. Yet, many families are separated by geographical boundaries, facing years of separation. Cherishing the privilege of being close to family and friends is essential. The emotional support and bonds we share with them are invaluable.

5. Opportunities and Pursuing Passions: A World of Choices

Employment opportunities and the ability to pursue our passions and dreams are privileges. Some people struggle to find work that sustains their livelihood or are stifled by societal norms that restrict their choices. Recognizing the freedom, we have to shape our careers and lives is vital.

In conclusion, it is crucial to count our blessings and express gratitude for the privileges we enjoy. By acknowledging these privileges, we can cultivate a mindset of gratitude, which not only enhances our own well-being but also motivates us to extend a helping hand to those less fortunate. Let us remember that, in appreciating what we have, we can make the world a better place for everyone.

52

Commitment to Goals

Overcoming Obstacles on the Journey

PSTO-52: It is incumbent on us to remain committed to the targets set by ourselves. Obstacles, if any enroute, may be treated as speed-breakers and may be negotiated suitably. Under no circumstances, it should deter or prevent us from reaching our desired destination.

In the pursuit of our goals and dreams, commitment plays a pivotal role. It is not merely about setting targets but also about unwavering determination to achieve them. Along the journey, obstacles are inevitable, but they should be viewed as speed-breakers rather than roadblocks. This essay will delve into the importance of commitment, emphasizing that obstacles should never deter us from reaching our desired destination, with the help of real-life examples.

1. The Power of Commitment

Commitment is the foundation of any successful endeavour. It's the driving force that propels us forward, even when the going gets tough. Jiro Ono, a legendary sushi master in Japan, faced numerous challenges in his pursuit of perfection in the art of sushi-making. Despite humble beginnings and a highly competitive industry, Jiro remained committed to his craft. His dedication to quality and precision led to the recognition of his restaurant, Sukiyabashi Jiro, as one of the best sushi establishments in the world. Jiro's story, portrayed in the documentary "Jiro Dreams of Sushi," exemplifies the importance of unwavering commitment and continuous improvement in the face of professional challenges.

2. Mindfulness and Compassionate Leadership

Jeff Weiner, the former CEO of LinkedIn, faced challenges related to professional burnout earlier in his career. Recognizing the importance of well-being and balance, Weiner made a commitment to prioritize mindfulness and compassionate leadership. He implemented changes in his own work habits and, as CEO, fostered a company culture that valued employee well-being. Weiner's commitment to creating a positive work environment showcases the transformative impact of personal commitment on organizational culture and success.

3. Resilience in the Face of Adversity

Commitment also entails resilience. When obstacles seem overwhelming, it's essential to draw strength from our commitment to the goal. We have already seen the story of Malala Yousafzai, or Michel Jordan or Bethany Hamilton or even J. K. Rowling. Despite facing a life-threatening or survival-scare scenario, they remained steadfast in their commitment and their resilience and unwavering dedication made them succeed.

In conclusion, in our pursuit of goals, commitment is our guiding star. Obstacles may appear, but they should never deter us from reaching our desired destination. Instead, we should view them as speed-breakers on the path to success. Drawing inspiration from individuals, we can understand that commitment, adaptability, and resilience are the keys to overcoming obstacles and achieving greatness. In the face of challenges, let us remain committed to our aspirations, for it is this commitment that will lead us to the fulfilment of our dreams.

53

The Universal Value of Respect

Embracing Diversity and Equality

PSTO-53: Everyone deserves respect, irrespective of social status or age or as it is always told, 'caste, creed or colour'. It is 'me & me only', who has to ensure it, on all occasions and all situations.

Respect, a fundamental human virtue, transcends boundaries and should be extended to every individual, regardless of their social status, age, or the factors of "caste, creed, or colour." It is a personal responsibility, one that each of us must uphold consistently, in all circumstances. This essay underscores the significance of respecting others, drawing inspiration from real-life examples that demonstrate the importance of this universal value.

1. Respect for All Ages: Bridging Generational Gaps

Age should never be a barrier to respect. The wisdom of the elderly and the enthusiasm of the youth deserve equal acknowledgment. Take, for instance, the story of 16-year-old Gitanjali Rao, who was named TIME magazine's Kid of the Year in 2020 for her innovative solutions to global problems. Her accomplishments showcase that respect knows no age, and young voices can have a profound impact when given the respect they deserve.

2. Fighting for Respect and Equality

Raja Ram Mohan Roy, the father of the Indian Renaissance, championed the cause of respect for all, fighting against social evils like Sati and caste-based discrimination. Despite strong opposition from orthodox groups, he believed it was his responsibility to ensure that every person, regardless of caste, gender, or religion, was treated with dignity. His relentless efforts led to the abolition of Sati and initiated social reforms that laid the foundation for equality in modern India.

3. Respect for Human Dignity

Irom Sharmila, the "Iron Lady of Manipur," embarked on a hunger strike to demand the repeal of the Armed Forces Special Powers Act (AFSPA), which gave unchecked power to the military. Despite facing oppression and continuous house arrest, she maintained that respect for human life and dignity should prevail regardless of caste, creed, or status. Her 16-year peaceful protest embodied the belief that every person deserves respect, and she ensured it by holding herself accountable for upholding these values.

4. Building a Harmonious Society

Respect serves as the cornerstone of a harmonious society. It fosters understanding, cooperation, and empathy. In a world marked by differences, respect for one another's unique qualities can lead to a more peaceful and inclusive world.

In conclusion, we all realise that Respect is a universal value that transcends social status, age, and the factors of "caste, creed, or colour." It is not only a societal expectation but also a personal responsibility. We should draw inspiration from individuals like Gitanjali Rao, Raja Ram Mohan Roy, and Irom Sharmila, who have championed the cause of respect and equality. In embracing diversity and upholding the principles of respect, we can build a more inclusive and harmonious world, where every individual is treated with the dignity and kindness they deserve.

54

Faces of Unshaken Trust

Guiding Our Giant Leaps of Faith

PSTO-54: We all come to a stage in life from where we may have to take a giant leap of faith. At that particular moment, the faces that flash before our eyes are of them on whom we have unshaken trust. Please count how many you see. That will define in what state of preparedness you are in.

Life often presents us with moments when we are required to take a giant leap of faith, stepping into the unknown. It is during these critical junctures that the faces of those we trust implicitly flash before our eyes, defining our state of preparedness. This essay delves into the significance of unshaken trust, drawing inspiration from real-life examples that highlight the pivotal role trust plays in our journeys.

1. Faith in the Team

Lewis Hamilton, a seven-time Formula 1 World Champion, often talks about the importance of trusting his racing crew. During key moments in races, where one wrong call can mean losing everything, Hamilton has had to take leaps of faith in his team's strategy and the engineers behind him. In those critical seconds, the people Hamilton trusts unconditionally—the team members who flash before his eyes—define his sense of preparedness and confidence to make those split-second decisions.

2. Trust in Crew

Kalpana Chawla, the first woman of Indian origin in space, took a monumental leap of faith when she embarked on her space missions with NASA. Space exploration requires immense trust in one's crew and mission control. During her time aboard the space shuttle, the faces of her team—fellow astronauts, engineers, and scientists whom she deeply trusted—would have been her pillars of faith. This trust allowed her to focus on the mission, knowing that her team had her back, defining her preparedness and resolve in the unknown realm of space.

3. Mentors and Guides: Guiding Lights

Mentors and guides play a crucial role in our journeys. The face of a trusted mentor, like Mahatma Gandhi's mentor Gopal Krishna Gokhale, can provide the guidance needed to navigate difficult paths. Gandhi's trust in Gokhale's wisdom and principles greatly influenced his life's work.

4. Self-Trust: The Foundation

While trust in others is essential, self-trust forms the foundation of all leaps of faith. Amelia Earhart, the first female aviator to fly solo across the Atlantic Ocean, had unshakable trust in her skills and abilities. Her face, in moments of doubt, was a reminder of her self-confidence.

Taking a giant leap of faith is a transformative moment in our lives. The faces that flash before our eyes in such moments represent the depth of trust we have in ourselves and others. Unshaken trust, whether in family, mentors, friends, or oneself, is the driving force that propels us forward. Drawing inspiration from the Lewis Hamilton, Kalpana Chawla, Mahatma Gandhi, Amelia Earhart, and countless others, we learn that trust is the cornerstone of courage and achievement. It is this trust that enables us to soar to new heights and achieve the extraordinary.

55

Resilience in the Pursuit of Dreams

Defining Moments of Perseverance

PSTO-55: While pursuing a dream, there may be many occasions when one feels like just giving up. But our precise reaction to that moment truly defines who we are and what material we are made of.

The pursuit of a dream is a journey filled with challenges, setbacks, and moments when giving up seems tempting. It is precisely in these critical moments that our reactions define our character and the substance of our being. This essay explores the concept of resilience in the pursuit of dreams, drawing inspiration from real-life examples that illustrate how our response to adversity shapes our path to success.

1. The Power of Perseverance

Perseverance is the unwavering determination to keep going, even in the face of seemingly insurmountable obstacles. We have already read the story of Arunima Sinha's journey to becoming the first female amputee to climb Mount Everest, which is a testament to her resilience and precise reaction in the face of life-altering adversity. After losing her leg in a tragic train accident, Arunima could have chosen to abandon her dream of mountaineering. However, her precise reaction to the moment of despair showcased her indomitable spirit. Instead of giving up, Arunima decided to pursue her dream with even greater determination. She underwent rigorous training, faced physical challenges, and overcame societal scepticism to achieve the extraordinary feat of reaching the summit of Mount Everest. Arunima's story is a powerful example of how one's response to adversity defines not only personal success but also inspires others facing similar challenges.

2. Defying Self-Doubt

Moments of self-doubt are natural when chasing dreams. Lionel Messi's journey to becoming one of the greatest footballers faced challenges early in his career due to his diminutive stature. His relatively small build led to doubts about his ability to succeed in a sport where physicality is often emphasized. However, Messi's precise reaction to these challenges defined his character and determination. Instead of giving in to doubt or succumbing to external pressures, Messi responded with unparalleled dedication to his craft. He embraced his unique playing style, showcasing extraordinary skill, agility, and goal-scoring prowess. Messi's precise reaction to moments of skepticism and adversity propelled him to numerous individual awards, record-breaking achievements, and a legacy as one of football's all-time greats. His story illustrates that how one responds to doubt and challenges is a crucial factor in achieving extraordinary success.

3. Turning Setbacks into Comebacks

Resilience means transforming setbacks into comebacks. The story of Walt Disney serves as a remarkable example. Disney faced bankruptcy and rejection numerous times while trying to establish Disneyland and Disney World. However, he turned these setbacks into opportunities, creating a legacy that continues to inspire generations.

4. A Test of Character

Moments when we contemplate giving up reveal our true character. Jim Carrey, the renowned actor and comedian, faced challenging circumstances early in his life. His family experienced financial difficulties, and Carrey had to drop out of school to support them. Despite these hardships, Carrey's precise reaction was one of determination and a commitment to his passion for comedy. He began performing at comedy clubs and eventually gained recognition for his unique comedic style. Carrey's resilience and precise reaction to adversity propelled him to become one of the most successful and beloved actors in Hollywood.

In conclusion, the pursuit of dreams is a test of character and resilience. Moments when giving up seems like an option are precisely the moments that define who we are. Drawing inspiration from individuals like Arunima Sinha, Lionel Messi, Walt Disney, and Jim Carrey, we learn that resilience is the key to transforming adversity into triumph. In these defining moments of perseverance, we discover our true strength and our capacity to achieve the extraordinary. The path to realizing our dreams is not always smooth, but it is navigating the rough patches that truly defines us.

56

Unsung Heroes

Acknowledging Those Who Make Our Lives Comfortable

PSTO-56: There are many people around us who, as per our understanding or perception may not be ensuring nay direct benefit to us. But they make it sure that we are not inconvenienced at any point of time. It could be the traffic police, or the garbage/sewage cleaner or the gardener in the park, so on and so forth. How many times have we stopped to thank them for making our life so comfortable and so beautiful?

In our daily lives, there are numerous individuals who may not provide us with direct benefits, yet they play crucial roles in ensuring our comfort and well-being. It could be the traffic police officer managing chaotic intersections, the garbage or sewage cleaner maintaining cleanliness, or the gardener nurturing the beauty of our parks. This chapter explores the importance of recognizing and thanking these unsung heroes who contribute to our comfort and the aesthetics of our surroundings, using real-life examples to highlight the significance of their roles.

1. The Traffic Police Officer: Safeguarding Order on the Roads

Traffic police officers are often taken for granted as they tirelessly manage traffic flow, ensuring our safety and convenience on the roads. Consider a congested intersection where a traffic cop's vigilant presence keeps chaos at bay. A simple "thank you" or a nod of appreciation can go a long way in recognizing their contribution to our daily lives.

2. Garbage and Sewage Cleaners: Guardians of Cleanliness

The individuals responsible for collecting garbage and maintaining sewage systems are often overlooked. Yet, their work ensures that our surroundings remain clean and free from health hazards. Acknowledging their efforts through a smile or a word of gratitude can brighten their day and remind them that their work matters.

3. Gardeners: Artists of Nature

Park gardeners are like artists who sculpt the beauty of our green spaces. Their meticulous care creates serene environments for us to enjoy. A simple "thank you" during a morning walk can make their tireless efforts feel worthwhile.

4. Utility Workers: Behind-the-Scenes Heroes

Utility workers, such as electricians, plumbers, and sanitation workers, are often unnoticed until we face a crisis. Recognizing their role in maintaining our comfort can foster a sense of community and appreciation.

5. Public Transport Staff: Keeping Us Moving

Public transport staff, from bus drivers to subway operators, enable us to commute efficiently. A polite thank you when boarding or alighting can make their long hours of service feel valued.

The individuals who work diligently to ensure our comfort and the beauty of our surroundings are the unsung heroes of our daily lives. While their roles may not directly benefit us in obvious ways, their contributions are invaluable. Taking a moment to express gratitude through a smile, a nod, or a simple "thank you" can go a long way in acknowledging their efforts and brightening their day. It's essential to remember that recognizing the contributions of these unsung heroes not only uplifts their spirits but also strengthens the bonds within our communities. In appreciating them, we create a more harmonious and caring society where every individual's efforts are acknowledged and valued.

57

The Power of Composure

Winning Arguments Through Logic and Patience

PSTO-57: Do we ever realise that we argue angrily, whenever we are in weak-footing? Angry utterances never help us win over anyone nor facilitate coming out successful an any argument. At the end of the day, it is our logic, knowledge, patience and perspective among many other, are the ones, which help to make a win-win situation.

In the heat of an argument, it's easy to resort to anger, especially when we feel on shaky ground. However, what we may not realize is that angry outbursts rarely lead to success. Instead, it is qualities like logic, knowledge, patience, and a balanced perspective that pave the way for fruitful discussions and win-win outcomes. This essay explores the significance of maintaining composure in arguments, using real-life examples to illustrate how these qualities can lead to successful and productive interactions.

1. The Role of Composure in Persuasion

Composure is a powerful tool in persuasion. Consider the example of Mahatma Gandhi, a symbol of peaceful resistance. He led

India to independence through nonviolent means, using logic, knowledge, and patience to convince the masses and British authorities of the merits of his cause. His composure in the face of adversity ultimately led to a win-win outcome for both sides.

2. Logic and Reason: Building Strong Arguments

Logic and reason are the cornerstones of compelling arguments. When we present our case calmly and logically, we make it easier for others to understand and accept our perspective. Carl Sagan, a renowned astrophysicist and science communicator, exemplified this through his ability to explain complex scientific concepts to the public in a clear, logical, and patient manner.

3. Calm Resolve in Women Empowerment

Mahadevi Verma, a prominent Hindi poetess and social activist, dealt with opposition during her time advocating for women's education and empowerment. Despite facing strong resistance from traditionalist circles, she never resorted to angry retorts or heated arguments. Instead, her calm demeanor, logical reasoning, and strong knowledge of the cultural landscape allowed her to win over people and create a space for women in Indian literature and education, proving that anger only weakens one's position.

3. Mastering the Art of Reason in Law

Fali Nariman, one of India's most respected constitutional lawyers, has shown throughout his career how patience and logic triumph over heated exchanges. Known for his calm and composed demeanor in court, Nariman has faced intense arguments without raising his voice or becoming angry. His success as a lawyer and mediator is a testament to the fact that sound reasoning, knowledge, and patience are the tools that win arguments, not anger.

4. Balanced Perspective: Finding Common Ground

A balanced perspective helps us identify common ground and

areas of agreement. In international diplomacy, leaders like Nelson Mandela, Atal Bihari Vajpayee and Kofi Annan used their diplomatic skills to bridge divides and find peaceful solutions to conflicts.

In arguments and discussions, maintaining composure and relying on qualities like logic, knowledge, patience, and a balanced perspective can lead to successful outcomes. The real-life examples of tall leaders like Mahatma Gandhi, Carl Sagan, Mahadevi Verma, Fali Nariman, Nelson Mandela, Atal Bihari Vajpayee and Kofi Annan demonstrate how these qualities can be powerful tools for positive change and conflict resolution. Instead of allowing anger to cloud our judgment and hinder productive dialogue, let us harness the power of these attributes to build bridges, foster understanding, and create win-win situations. In doing so, we not only achieve our goals but also contribute to a more harmonious and cooperative world.

58

The Power of Visualization

A Roadmap to Achievement

PSTO-58: The first few steps to any action would be to sit back and think about it. I have always felt that a mental picture of the task to be accomplished and the perceived feeling of joy on its achievement give us the initial push to go for it.

Before embarking on any journey, it is often essential to take a moment to sit back, contemplate, and visualize the task at hand. Creating a mental picture of the goal and experiencing the joy of its achievement can be the catalyst for taking the initial steps. This essay explores the concept of visualization as a powerful tool for motivation and action, using real-life examples to illustrate how this practice can set the stage for success.

1. The Importance of Mental Preparation

Mental preparation is the first step toward accomplishing any task. Sir Edmund Hillary and Tenzing Norgay, the first climbers to reach the summit of Mount Everest, did not embark on their expedition without meticulous planning and mental visualization. They mentally rehearsed their ascent, overcoming obstacles in their minds long before they faced them in reality.

2. Visionary Leadership

Sundar Pichai, known for his role in leading Google, often speaks about the importance of setting a vision and imagining the future he wants to create for the company. Before embarking on major projects, Pichai takes time to visualize the impact of their innovations on users worldwide. This mental exercise helps him align his team's efforts toward achieving transformative goals while fostering a sense of shared purpose.

3. Harnessing the Power of Positive Emotions

Visualization is not just about the image; it's also about experiencing the emotions associated with success. When we feel the joy, satisfaction, and fulfilment of achieving our goals in our minds, we are more motivated to take action. Serena Williams, one of the greatest tennis players of all time, often visualized winning Grand Slam titles and feeling the euphoria of victory. This mental rehearsal fuelled her determination and drive on the court.

4. Power of Positive Visualisation

Shiv Khera, a well-known motivational speaker, emphasizes the importance of visualization in achieving success. In his workshops, he encourages participants to imagine their goals vividly, focusing on the joy and satisfaction they would feel upon achieving them. By promoting this mental imagery, he helps individuals break through mental barriers and take actionable steps toward their aspirations.

Visualization is a potent tool that sets the stage for action and achievement. By mentally preparing ourselves and creating vivid mental pictures of our goals, we tap into a wellspring of motivation and determination. The examples of Sir Edmund Hillary and Tenzing Norgay, Sundar Pichai, Serena Williams, and Shiv Khera demonstrate how visualization can be a driving force behind remarkable accomplishments. It not only helps us clarify our objectives but also fuels our passion and perseverance. In essence, visualization transforms dreams into realities and serves as a roadmap to success in all our endeavors.

59

Counting Blessings

Shaping Your Future with Gratitude

PSTO-59: Never forget to count the blessings you receive in your journey of life. They would define how your future would be.

In the journey of life, it's easy to get caught up in pursuing future aspirations and forget to count the blessings we receive along the way. However, these blessings are not just momentary gifts; they shape our attitudes, outlooks, and the very trajectory of our future. This essay delves into the importance of counting our blessings and practicing gratitude, using real-life examples to illustrate how this mindset can shape a brighter future.

1. Gratitude as a Perspective Shifter

Gratitude is a perspective shifter that enables us to appreciate the present moment. Consider the story of Anne Frank, a Jewish girl who found solace in writing during the Holocaust. Despite the dire circumstances, her diary reflects her ability to count her blessings, finding hope and beauty in the midst of darkness.

2. Overcoming Mental Health Struggle

Michael Phelps, the most decorated Olympian of all time, faced severe mental health struggles despite his success. Phelps has spoken about how being grateful for his blessings—both in terms of career achievements and personal growth—helped him regain balance in life. His gratitude for both triumphs and challenges allowed him to define his future beyond the pool, becoming an advocate for mental health awareness.

3. Advocacy fro Incarcerated Ones

Kiran Bedi, the first woman to join the Indian Police Service (IPS), frequently speaks about counting her blessings, particularly her education and early support from her parents. These advantages allowed her to break barriers and become a leader in social reform. Bedi's gratitude has driven her to work tirelessly for prison reform and women's rights, creating a ripple effect of positive change in society.

4. Gratitude for Longevity and Support

Roger Federer, considered one of the greatest tennis players in history, often speaks about how he counts his blessings, particularly in terms of the longevity of his career and the support from his fans, family, and team. Federer acknowledges that his career could have ended early due to injuries, but his gratitude for his health, family, and opportunities has helped shape his future, both on and off the court. His humble attitude and recognition of his blessings have played a key role in his enduring legacy.

5. Acknowledgement

Acknowledging that gratitude can be a powerful motivator for success, is in itself a tool for the same. Will Smith, a successful actor and producer, often speaks about the importance of gratitude and hard work. He attributes his achievements to a positive mindset and acknowledges the role of blessings in his life. Will Smith emphasizes the need to appreciate the journey, learn from experiences, and express gratitude for the opportunities that arise.

In conclusion, counting our blessings and practicing gratitude are not mere gestures of politeness; they have the power to shape our future. The stories of Anne Frank, Michael Phelp, Kiran Bedi, Roger Federer, and Will Smith illustrate how gratitude can transform our perspectives, build resilience, foster positive relationships, and motivate us to achieve great things. By recognizing the blessings we receive, no matter how small, we cultivate a mindset that leads to a brighter and more fulfilling future. Gratitude is not just an action; it is a way of life that enriches our experiences and leaves a lasting legacy of positivity and hope.

60

Embracing Impermanence

A Reminder in the Pursuit of Meaning

PSTO-60: How many of us do not know that nothing is permanent in life? None, I am sure. Yet, most of us forget it in a hurry in our quest for materialism and pseudo success.

The impermanence of life is a truth we all inherently know, yet it's a lesson we often overlook in our relentless pursuit of materialism and superficial success. This chapter explores the profound concept of impermanence, highlighting how recognizing its reality can lead to a deeper, more meaningful existence. We will draw inspiration from real-life examples that demonstrate the transformative power of this awareness.

1. The Illusion of Materialism

Materialism often lures us into believing that possessions and achievements can provide lasting happiness. However, consider the story of Howard Hughes, a billionaire known for his extravagant lifestyle. Despite his immense wealth, he lived a reclusive and unfulfilled life, emphasizing that material possessions are fleeting and can't guarantee lasting contentment.

2. Embracing Impermanence in Business

Ratan Tata, the renowned Indian industrialist, has often spoken about how nothing in life, including success or failure, is permanent. He faced significant challenges during his tenure at Tata Group, including the Nano car project, which failed to meet its expectations. Despite setbacks, Tata's acceptance of impermanence helped him make bold decisions, knowing that both success and failure are transient phases in the larger journey of life.

3. Transience in Nature

Nature itself teaches us the lesson of impermanence. Cherry blossoms, for example, bloom in all their glory for a brief period each year. Their ephemeral beauty reminds us that even the most exquisite moments are fleeting. Learning to appreciate the beauty in impermanence can lead to a richer appreciation of life.

4. Understanding Life Beyond Fame

Michael Jordan, one of the greatest basketball players in history, came to terms with the fact that fame and success on the court were not permanent. Post-retirement, Jordan transitioned into business and philanthropy, understanding that the quest for materialistic success doesn't define long-term fulfilment. His career and life transitions show how he embraced the concept that nothing is permanent, allowing him to navigate life with a balanced perspective.

5. The Quest for Inner Fulfilment

The pursuit of inner fulfilment, rather than external validation, can lead to a more meaningful life. Viktor Frankl, a Holocaust survivor and psychiatrist, wrote about finding purpose and meaning even in the most challenging circumstances. He emphasized that our ability to choose our response to life's impermanence is where our true power lies.

In conclusion, the impermanence of life is an undeniable truth that we often forget in our quest for materialism and superficial success. Real-life examples like Howard Hughes, Ratan Tata, Michael Jordan, and Viktor Frankl remind us that true fulfilment is found in recognizing the transient nature of existence and seeking meaning beyond the ephemeral. Embracing impermanence can lead us to a deeper appreciation of life's beauty, a greater capacity for resilience, and a quest for enduring meaning. It is a reminder that, in the face of life's uncertainties, we have the power to choose a path of purpose and fulfilment.

61

Life's One-Off Events

Lessons, Not Definitions

PSTO-61: We must consider a happening in our life as just a one-off event. They neither define us nor our future. We have to just learn from it and move on.

In the tapestry of our lives, there are moments that stand out as one-off events, neither defining us nor determining our future. These unique occurrences, whether positive or negative, are valuable opportunities for learning and growth. This chapter delves into the idea that life's one-off events should be seen as lessons rather than defining moments, using real-life examples to illustrate the wisdom of this perspective.

1. Overcoming from Form Slumps

Virat Kohli, known for his immense success as a cricketer, has faced numerous rough patches, particularly his form slump in 2021-22. However, Kohli consistently emphasizes that individual failures or bad performances do not define his career. His ability to move on from these phases and refocus on the present has been key to his resilience and ongoing success in the sport.

2. A Single Success Story

Like failure, Success itself can be a one-off event. Take, for instance, the story of Christopher Columbus, whose discovery of the Americas was a monumental achievement. Yet, his subsequent struggles and challenges in managing the newfound territory reveal that even great successes do not determine an entire life's course.

3. The Rise of Usain Bolt

Early in Usain Bolt's career, he faced setbacks and criticism for his performance. At the 2004 Athens Olympics, Bolt, then 17 years old, experienced a hamstring injury that forced him to withdraw from the competition. This setback could have been discouraging for a young athlete, but Bolt used it as a learning opportunity.

Rather than letting the injury define him, Bolt worked on improving his strength, technique, and overall fitness. He dedicated himself to rigorous training under coach Glen Mills and focused on perfecting his sprinting skills. This period of setback and subsequent hard work set the stage for Bolt's remarkable success in the years that followed.

In the 2008 Beijing Olympics, Bolt not only redeemed himself but also stunned the world. He won three gold medals and set world records in the 100 meters, 200 meters, and 4x100 meters relay. Bolt's ability to view the setback in Athens as a one-off event, learn from it, and then achieve unprecedented success demonstrated his resilience and determination.

Life's one-off events are like pages in a book, each with its own lesson and purpose. They should neither define us nor limit our potential. Instead, they offer opportunities for learning, growth, and transformation. The stories of Virat Kohli, Christopher Columbus, and Usain Bolt demonstrate that even the most significant one-off events are but a part of a larger narrative. By embracing these events as lessons and moving forward with resilience and determination, we can shape our own stories and create meaningful futures. Life is not defined by a single event; it is defined by how we respond to and learn from them.

62

Speaking Up for Others

The Priceless Virtue

PSTO-62: It's often told Silence is Golden. Yet to me, "Speaking up for others" is perhaps beyond diamond. We must utilise it fully whenever such opportunity knocks.

While it's often said that "silence is golden" there are moments when speaking up for others transcends any precious metal or gem. This act of advocacy and support is a testament to our empathy, compassion, and moral responsibility. This chapter explores the profound significance of speaking up for others, highlighting how seizing such opportunities can lead to positive change. Real-life examples will illustrate the transformative impact of this virtue.

1. Speaking for Marginalised Voices

Arundhati Roy, an Indian author and activist, has consistently spoken up for marginalized and oppressed communities, even when silence would have been the easier path. Through her books and activism, she has highlighted social and political injustices in India and globally. Roy exemplifies the belief that speaking up for others is invaluable, making her voice a powerful tool for social change.

2. Promoting Social Justice

Advocacy for others plays a pivotal role in promoting social justice. Rosa Parks, often referred to as the "mother of the civil rights movement," refused to give up her bus seat to a white passenger, sparking the Montgomery Bus Boycott. Her simple act of speaking up catalysed a nationwide movement for racial equality.

3. Supporting the Vulnerable

As a successful actress, Emma Watson could have chosen to enjoy her career success in the entertainment industry without delving into social and feminist issues. However, Watson became a UN Women Goodwill Ambassador and launched the HeForShe campaign, advocating for gender equality. She used her platform to speak up against sexism and discrimination. Watson's commitment to gender equality and her outspoken advocacy transcends the material success of her acting career, making her a prominent voice for social change. Watson utilizes her fame to bring attention to gender inequality and continues to work towards creating a more inclusive and equal world.

4. Creating Inclusive Communities

Speaking up for others fosters inclusive communities. Harvey Milk, the first openly gay elected official in California, used his platform to advocate for LGBTQ+ rights. His activism and vocal support paved the way for greater acceptance and equality.

5. Championing Human Rights

Speaking up for others is a cornerstone of championing human rights. Eleanor Roosevelt, former First Lady of the United States, was a driving force behind the Universal Declaration of Human Rights. Her advocacy shaped international human rights standards and protections.

In conclusion, "Speaking up for others" is a virtue that transcends the idea that "silence is golden." It is an act of empathy, compassion, and moral responsibility. The stories of Arundhati Roy, Rosa Parks, Emma Watson, Harvey Milk, and Eleanor Roosevelt demonstrate that speaking up can lead to transformative change, from saving lives and promoting social justice to supporting the vulnerable and championing human rights. In a world where injustice and inequality persist, our voices have the power to inspire positive action, challenge norms, and create inclusive and compassionate societies. Speaking up for others is a reminder that our voices can be instruments of profound change and progress.

63

The Quest for Perfect Solutions

Rediscovering the Power of Fundamentals

PSTO-63: How often have we realized that solution was just around, yet it eluded us? Is it not that in our quest for a perfect solution, we tend to ignore basics or the fundamentals? We must introspect on it often, I guess.

In our relentless pursuit of perfect solutions, we often overlook the simplicity and effectiveness of fundamentals. It's a common experience to realize that the answer was right there, within reach, yet eluded us due to our focus on complexity. This chapter delves into the importance of introspection and the recognition of the power of fundamentals in problem-solving, using real-life examples to illustrate the wisdom of this perspective.

1. The Elegance of Simplicity

Simplicity is often the hallmark of ingenious solutions. A.R. Rahman, the renowned composer and music maestro, faced a challenge during the creation of the soundtrack for the movie "Roja." He was struggling to find the perfect musical theme that captured the essence of the film. In his quest for perfection, Rahman found himself exploring complex compositions and intricate melodies. However, the breakthrough came when he revisited the basics. He stumbled upon a simple tune that resonated with the emotions of the film. Rahman's experience in creating the "Roja" soundtrack taught him the importance of introspection and revisiting the fundamentals. The solution was not in complexity but in the essence of simplicity. This realization influenced his future approach to music composition, emphasizing the power of basic elements in creating memorable and impactful melodies.

2. Back to the Basics in Medicine

In the medical field, the fundamentals are the foundation of diagnosis and treatment. Dr. Paul Farmer, a global health leader, emphasizes the importance of basics like clean water and sanitation in improving global health. His organization, Partners in Health, has successfully addressed complex health challenges by prioritizing simple, fundamental solutions.

3. Fundamentals in Sports

Fundamentals play a crucial role in sports. The legendary basketball coach John Wooden, who led the UCLA Bruins to ten NCAA championships, stressed the importance of mastering the basics. He believed that a strong foundation in fundamentals was the key to success in any endeavour.

4. Looking for that Elusive Solution Around

It is many times true that solutions could be just round the corner, yet eluding us. Viswanathan Anand, the Indian chess grandmaster, faced a critical moment during the World Chess Championship in 2010. He was competing against Veselin Topalov and was struggling to find a winning move in a crucial game. Anand, in his pursuit of a perfect move, was initially overlooking a fundamental principle in chess—pawn structures. The solution to the position was rooted in a basic understanding of the pawn structure on the board. Anand, after some reflection, realized that he had momentarily ignored the basics of chess strategy in his intense focus on finding a complex winning move. Embracing this realization, he made a move based on fundamental principles, leading to victory in that critical game and eventually securing the World Chess Championship.

The pursuit of perfect solutions can sometimes blind us to the elegance and effectiveness of fundamentals. The examples of A.R. Rahman, Dr. Paul Farmer, John Wooden, and Viswanathan Anand illustrate that simplicity and a focus on basics can lead to ingenious solutions, breakthroughs, and innovation. It is a reminder that introspection is essential in problem-solving. By taking a step back, reevaluating our approach, and embracing the power of fundamentals, we can uncover elegant, efficient, and effective solutions that were often right in front of us. The quest for perfection should not overshadow the timeless wisdom of the basics.

64

Discovering Happiness

Embracing the Reasons the World Provides

PSTO-64: World provides us many reasons to be happy. It's incumbent on us to recognize and build on those.

In a world filled with both challenges and opportunities, happiness is a treasure often found in recognizing and building upon the countless reasons the world provides. This chapter explores the profound concept of finding joy in everyday moments and circumstances. It emphasizes the importance of recognizing the sources of happiness that surround us, using real-life examples to illustrate the transformative impact of this perspective.

1. Laughter, Kindness and Inclusivity

The sources of happiness could be many, which needs to be looked around. Ellen DeGeneres, the comedian and talk show host, faced challenges in her career, including the public reaction to her coming out as gay. Despite this, she recognized the importance of laughter, kindness, and inclusivity as sources of happiness. Ellen actively built on these sources of happiness by creating "The Ellen DeGeneres

Show," a platform known for its positive and entertaining content. Her commitment to spreading joy, kindness, and laughter made her a beloved figure in the entertainment industry, showcasing how she built on the recognition of happiness in simple yet impactful ways.

2. Pioneering Cancer Care

Dr. V. Shanta, a pioneer in cancer care at the Adyar Cancer Institute in Chennai, found happiness in bringing hope to cancer patients and their families. She recognized the joy in helping others, even in dire circumstances, and dedicated her life to providing affordable cancer care. By building on this source of happiness, she transformed cancer treatment in India and brought solace to countless lives.

3. Finding the Joy and Purpose

Many a times, we ignore the joy and purpose, which is already associated with whatever we do. Keanu Reeves, the actor known for his roles in iconic films, has faced personal tragedies and challenges throughout his life. Despite this, he recognizes the joy and purpose that comes from his love for acting, connecting with fans, and engaging in creative endeavours. Keanu actively builds on these reasons by approaching his career with humility and a positive attitude. He also involved himself in various charitable acts, including supporting cancer research and children's hospitals. Keanu's kindness, generosity, and dedication to his craft showcase how he builds on the recognition of happiness in both his professional and personal life.

4. Pursuit of Passions

Pursuing passions and interests can lead to a deep sense of happiness. Julia Child, a culinary icon, found her joy in French cuisine and cooking. Her passion not only enriched her life but also inspired countless others to explore their interests and discover their own reasons to be happy.

5. Creating Moments of Joy

Sometimes, happiness is a result of creating moments of joy intentionally. John Krasinski, during the COVID-19 pandemic, started the "Some Good News" web series to share positive stories and moments of happiness. His initiative reminded people that even in challenging times, we can find reasons to smile and celebrate.

Happiness is not an elusive treasure; it is a state of mind cultivated by recognizing and building upon the reasons the world provides. The stories of Ellen, Dr. V. Shanta, Keanu Reeves, Julia Child, and John Krasinski illustrate that happiness can be found in understanding the sources, a connection with nature, finding the joy and purpose, the pursuit of passions, and intentional efforts to create moments of joy. It is a reminder that, no matter the circumstances, the world offers a tapestry of reasons to be happy. By embracing these sources of happiness, we not only enrich our own lives but also inspire others to discover and cherish their own reasons for joy. Happiness is not something to be pursued; it is something to be recognized and nurtured within ourselves and the world around us.

65

Embracing Life's Whys

Finding Meaning in Adversity

PSTO-65: When something very good happens to us, we don't question, "Why me?" Then why is it that in times of adverse happening, our first question is' "Why me?"

When something positive occurs in our lives, we often don't question, "Why me?" Yet, in times of adversity, it's common to ask, "Why me?" This chapter explores the dichotomy between these questions, delving into the human experience of adversity and the profound lessons it offers. Real-life examples illustrate the transformative power of seeking meaning in challenging circumstances.

1. Celebrating Life's Blessings during Adversity

People who celebrate the life's blessings even in adversity are the ones, who do not question "why me". For ace Indian cricketer Yuvraj Singh, everything was going great. But, in 2011, he was diagnosed with a rare form of lung cancer, known as mediastinal seminoma. It was the peak of his cricket career. This shocking revelation brought an abrupt halt to his professional and personal life. Instead of asking, "Why me?" Yuvraj Singh embraced the challenge head-on. He opted for aggressive treatment, including chemotherapy sessions in the United States. The treatment was physically and emotionally gruelling, but Yuvraj faced it with remarkable courage and a positive attitude. During his cancer treatment, Yuvraj chose to share his journey with the public. This decision not only garnered widespread support but also raised awareness about cancer, its treatments, and the importance of early detection. Yuvraj Singh's journey through cancer treatment was a testament to his resilience. After months of battling the disease and undergoing intensive therapy, he successfully defeated cancer. His comeback to professional cricket was a triumphant moment, and he went on to represent the Indian cricket team once again. Yuvraj Singh's cancer journey teaches us that adversity does not discriminate, and even in the face of life-threatening challenges, one can find strength and resilience. Rather than dwelling on the question of "Why me?" Yuvraj focused on his recovery, creating awareness, and giving back to the community. Yuvraj Singh's openness about his cancer battle has inspired many facing similar challenges. His story serves as a beacon of hope, encouraging individuals to face adversity with determination and a positive mindset. Yuvraj Singh's cancer phase is a remarkable example of how one can navigate the darkest moments of life with courage, positivity, and a commitment to making a difference in the lives of others. His journey stands as a testament to the human spirit's ability to rise above adversity and find meaning in the face of life-altering challenges.

2. The Paradox of Adversity

Adversity often leads us to ask, "Why me?" It is a natural reaction to pain, loss, or unexpected challenges. Viktor Frankl, a Holocaust survivor and psychiatrist, delved into the paradox of adversity. He found that those who could find meaning in their suffering were more resilient and better equipped to overcome their challenges.

The questions "Why me?" in moments of adversity and "Why not me?" in moments of happiness reveal the complex nature of the human experience. While it's natural to ask "Why me?" in challenging times, seeking meaning and purpose in adversity can lead to resilience, growth, and positive change. The detailed example of Yuvraj Singh and Viktor Frankl demonstrate that adversity is not a punishment but an opportunity to find meaning, cultivate empathy, and make a lasting impact. Instead of dwelling on the question "Why me?" during tough times, we can shift our perspective to "What can I learn from this?" and "How can I use this experience to create a better world?" In doing so, we find profound answers to life's most challenging questions.

66

The Power of Gratitude

Transforming Lives with One 'Thank You' at a Time

PSTO-66: How many of us make it a point to express our gratitude to the people, who make a difference to our life? Expressing it brings in such a positive change in the entire atmosphere around us that we ourselves can feel energised too. It's definitely worth trying. Isn't it?

Expressing gratitude to those who make a difference in our lives is a practice that not only brightens someone else's day but also radiates positivity in our surroundings. This chapter explores the impact of gratitude and the transformative effect it has on both the giver and the receiver. Real-life examples illustrate the value of incorporating this practice into our daily lives.

1. The Ripple Effect of Gratitude

Taylor Swift, the Grammy-winning singer-songwriter, often expresses gratitude to her fans, collaborators, and supporters. She acknowledges the role they play in her career and success. Taylor's expressions of gratitude contribute to a positive fan base and industry relationships. By openly appreciating her fans and those she works with, she creates an atmosphere of mutual respect and support. Taylor Swift's gratitude is not just a formality but a genuine effort to connect with her audience and collaborators. This connection strengthens her bond with fans and fosters a positive and loyal community.

2. Enhancing Personal Well-being

Gratitude enhances personal well-being. Dr. Robert Emmons, a leading researcher on gratitude, has found that practicing gratitude can lead to improved mental and physical health. When we express gratitude, we shift our focus from what we lack to what we have, leading to increased happiness and overall life satisfaction.

3. Acknowledging Unsung Heroes

Gratitude acknowledges unsung heroes. Public servants like firefighters, healthcare workers, and educators often go unrecognized for their tireless efforts. When communities express their gratitude through acts of kindness or thank-you notes, it uplifts the spirits of these individuals and fosters a sense of unity and appreciation.

4. Inspiring Acts of Kindness

Gratitude inspires acts of kindness. In the wake of natural disasters, communities often come together to support one another. The outpouring of gratitude and assistance demonstrates how expressing thanks can mobilize people to make a positive difference in the lives of others.

Gratitude is a powerful force that has the capacity to transform lives and entire communities. The stories of Taylor Swift, Dr. Robert Emmons, and the collective response to disasters illustrate the value of expressing thanks. By taking the time to acknowledge and appreciate the efforts of those who make a difference in our lives, we not only bring positivity to our surroundings but also experience personal growth and well-being. Gratitude is a simple yet profoundly impactful practice that is worth incorporating into our daily lives. It reminds us that a "thank you" can be a small act with immeasurable consequences, creating a more compassionate and harmonious world for all.

67

Opportunities Knock

Transforming Challenges into Triumphs

PSTO-67: It is often told opportunity knocks only once. If we look at our lives, we may find many. It is just how we look at it. Converting challenges into opportunities, could be one such.

The adage "opportunity knocks only once" is a familiar saying, but upon closer examination, one realizes that life presents us with numerous opportunities, often camouflaged as challenges. In this chapter, the idea of converting challenges into opportunities is explored. The chapter also highlights how a shift in perspective can lead to remarkable triumphs. Real-life examples serve as compelling illustrations of this transformative process.

1. The Alchemy of Adversity

J.R.R. Tolkien, the renowned author of "The Lord of the Rings" trilogy, faced personal and professional challenges, including the loss of close friends during World War I and the struggles of academic life. Tolkien turned to creativity as a form of catharsis and a way to process his experiences. He transformed the challenges he faced into opportunities to create an entire fictional world with rich mythology and storytelling. Tolkien's ability to channel personal challenges into creative endeavours not only produced one of the most beloved fantasy series but also left a lasting literary legacy that continues to captivate readers worldwide.

2. Innovation Born from Necessity

Necessity has long been the mother of invention. During World War II, the scarcity of rubber led to the development of synthetic rubber by scientists like Charles Goodyear. This challenge transformed into an opportunity to create new materials with diverse applications, from tires to medical devices.

3. Overcoming Personal Trials

Challenges can also be deeply personal. Helen Keller, deaf and blind from an early age, turned her life's adversities into opportunities for learning and advocacy. Her remarkable journey exemplifies how one can overcome seemingly insurmountable challenges and inspire others in the process.

4. Turning Economic Downturns into Entrepreneurship

Economic challenges can spark entrepreneurial innovation. Howard Schultz, the founder of Starbucks, saw an opportunity during an economic downturn in the 1980s. He transformed traditional coffee shops into welcoming spaces for community and connection, building a global coffee empire.

5. Professional Challenges as a Call to Action

Jeff Immelt, former CEO of General Electric (GE), took the helm during a challenging period marked by the global financial crisis and shifts in the energy industry. Immelt viewed these challenges as opportunities for transformation and innovation. Under his leadership, GE diversified its portfolio, emphasizing technology and digital initiatives, showcasing his ability to turn challenges into opportunities for organizational change. Immelt's approach highlights the importance of adaptability in the face of challenges. By embracing change, he sought to position GE for future success, demonstrating the transformative impact of a proactive mindset.

The belief that "opportunity knocks only once" can be limiting. Challenges, whether personal or societal, often serve as fertile ground for innovation and growth. The stories of Tolkien, Charles Goodyear, Helen Keller, Howard Schultz, and Jeff Immelt demonstrate that converting challenges into opportunities is not only possible but can lead to remarkable triumphs. It requires a shift in perspective, resilience, and an open mind to recognize the potential in adversity. As we face challenges in our own lives, we should remember that each obstacle presents a unique opportunity for growth, learning, and the creation of a brighter future. By embracing challenges as stepping stones to success, we can transform adversity into opportunity, turning life's knocks into resounding triumphs.

68

Climbing Together

Making the Journey Up the Ladder More Enjoyable

PSTO-68: We all know that climbing a ladder is difficult, time-consuming, and energy-intensive too. Can we try on making it less cumbersome, more enjoyable, more memorable by having all the fellow-climbers, sharing the same passion and same joy in their efforts too? We must ponder over it. Isn't it?

Climbing the ladder of success can be a challenging and demanding journey. However, what if we could transform this ascent into a more enjoyable, memorable, and collaborative experience by sharing our passion and joy with fellow climbers? This chapter explores the idea of making the journey less cumbersome and more rewarding through collective efforts and camaraderie. Examples from real-life illustrate the transformative power of this perspective.

1. The Joy of Shared Passions

Pursuing a passion becomes even more fulfilling when shared with like-minded individuals. The Beatles, one of the most iconic music bands in history, shared a deep passion for music. Their collaboration not only produced timeless songs but also made their journey up the ladder of fame an immensely enjoyable and memorable experience.

2. Collective Efforts in Innovation

Innovation often thrives when individuals with diverse skills collaborate. The Wright brothers, Orville and Wilbur, shared a passion for aviation. Their collaborative efforts led to the invention of the first powered, controlled, and sustained flight, revolutionizing the world of transportation.

3. Supporting Each Other's Growth

Climbing the ladder together means providing support and encouragement. In the world of sports, there have been numerous examples. In recent times, we may take the case of Jürgen Klopp, the former Liverpool coach, who exemplified the power of mutual growth in his team. Known for his charismatic leadership, Klopp fostered a culture of unity, where every player supported one another's development. He emphasized that success wasn't just about individual brilliance but collective effort. By instilling a strong belief in teamwork, Klopp helped Liverpool players elevate each other, leading them to historic achievements, including a Premier League and Champions League title. His leadership shows that mutual support fuels both individual and team growth.

4. Creating a Positive Work Environment

In the workplace, a collaborative and supportive atmosphere can make the climb more enjoyable. Companies like Google prioritize teamwork and employee well-being. By fostering a sense of community and shared purpose, they enhance both individual and collective achievements.

5. Community and Mentorship

Many successful entrepreneurs find mentorship and community to be essential. Y. Combinator, a startup accelerator, provides a platform for founders to learn from experienced mentors and connect with fellow entrepreneurs. This collaborative environment helps startups thrive.

Climbing the ladder of success doesn't have to be a solitary or arduous journey. The stories of The Beatles, the Wright brothers, Jürgen Klopp, Google, and Y. Combinator illustrate the transformative power of shared passions, collective efforts, and supportive communities. By embracing collaboration, camaraderie, and the joy of pursuing shared goals, we can make the journey more enjoyable, memorable, and rewarding. It's a reminder that success need not be a lonely endeavour; it can be a collective and enriching experience. As we ponder over this idea, we realize that when we climb together, we not only reach greater heights but also create lasting bonds and cherished memories along the way.

69

Balancing Act

The Essential Harmony of Work and Relaxation

PSTO-69: As much as Work is necessary for us, so is Relaxation. Rejuvenating our body and mind gives us the required energy to pursue our passion, our goal. Everyone will have her/his own ways of relaxation. We must find ours soon, if not already done. It is never too late to refuel our body, our mind and our soul from time to time.

In the pursuit of our goals and passions, we often forget the vital counterpart to work; relaxation. The act of rejuvenating our body and mind is not a luxury but a necessity, providing the energy and clarity required for success. This chapter explores the importance of finding one's own relaxation methods and emphasizes that it is never too late to refuel our body, mind, and soul. Real-life examples underscore the significance of this balance.

1. Focus on Recovery and Relaxation

Abhinav Bindra's journey highlights the profound connection between mental health and performance in sports. After winning India's first individual Olympic gold medal at the Beijing 2008

Olympics, Bindra faced unexpected loneliness and mental health struggles. He candidly stated, "I would like to tell every athlete to ensure that their well-being as a human is at the heart of their performance. Tuning in to your own mental health and well-being is essential. And, of course, if any athlete is struggling, I would encourage them to seek help. There is absolutely no shame, and it is not a sign of weakness. It is a sign of great strength to seek help to get better." To regain his focus and clarity, Bindra turned to relaxation techniques. Bindra's commitment to mental well-being and relaxation has been essential in overcoming challenges, reinforcing the idea that rejuvenating our body and mind provides the necessary energy to pursue our passions and goals.

2. The Art of Mindfulness

Mindfulness practices are valuable tools for relaxation. Jon Kabat-Zinn, a pioneer in the field of mindfulness-based stress reduction, has helped countless individuals find peace and balance through mindfulness meditation. His work illustrates the transformative potential of these relaxation techniques.

3. Mental Health Advocacy

Naomi Osaka, a multi-time Grand Slam champion, made headlines when she prioritized her mental health by stepping away from several high-profile tennis tournaments. Osaka has openly discussed the importance of relaxation and mental well-being, taking time off to rejuvenate her mind and body. Her decision brought global attention to the idea that athletes, like everyone else, need time to recharge in order to pursue their goals with passion and focus.

The pursuit of our passions and goals should not come at the expense of relaxation and rejuvenation. The stories of Abhinav Bindra, Jon Kabat-Zinn, Naomi Osaka, & Serena Williams highlight the various paths to relaxation, from nature and mindfulness to creative expression, physical wellness, and cultural exploration. It is a reminder that finding our own relaxation methods is essential for maintaining the delicate balance between work and well-being. It is never too late to refuel our body, mind, and soul. By prioritizing relaxation, we not only enhance our ability to pursue our passions and goals but also lead more fulfilling and harmonious lives. In the intricate dance of life, balance is the key to sustained success and lasting happiness.

70

Finding Growth in every Experience

Embracing the Reality

PSTO-70: Every occurrence in our lives comes with its 'ifs & buts'. However, when we have a relook at the same event after passage of time, on most occasions we realize that it made a substantive positive impact on our lives. Hence, it is incumbent on us to understand it and take the best out of every moment.

Life is a series of events that come with their own uncertainties and challenges—our "ifs and buts." Yet, when we take the time to reflect on these moments, we often realize that even the most difficult experiences have led to significant personal growth or positive outcomes. Understanding this can empower us to embrace every situation as a potential catalyst for change.

1. Embracing Change and Adaptability

Life is filled with unexpected changes, and those who adapt often find new opportunities for growth. A notable example is Sunil Gavaskar, a legendary cricketer who initially thrived in the traditional format of Test cricket. However, as the game evolved with the introduction of One Day Internationals (ODIs) and T20 formats, Gavaskar embraced these changes, adapting his style and approach to succeed in the shorter formats. His willingness to evolve not only extended his career but also set a precedent for future cricketers. Gavaskar's journey shows that embracing change can lead to unforeseen benefits and continued success.

2. Learning from Failure

The Indian Space Research Organisation's (ISRO) Chandrayaan missions exemplify how learning from failure can lead to remarkable success. The first Chandrayaan mission faced challenges, but the insights gained paved the way for the successful Chandrayaan-2. Each setback contributed to ISRO's knowledge and capabilities, ultimately leading to significant advancements in space exploration. This illustrates that reflecting on failures can yield valuable lessons that drive future achievements.

3. Cultivating Resilience

The life of Abraham Lincoln is a powerful testament to resilience. Throughout his journey, he faced numerous defeats and setbacks, including multiple electoral losses and personal tragedies. Yet, his unwavering determination and belief in his vision led him to become one of America's greatest presidents. Lincoln's ability to persist despite adversity demonstrates how cultivating resilience can enable us to overcome challenges and achieve greatness.

4. Finding Purpose in Adversity

The story of Baji Rout, a young boy from Odisha, highlights how adversity can inspire profound purpose. At just 12 years old, Baji sacrificed his life while resisting British colonial forces, embodying bravery and selflessness. His actions sparked a sense of nationalism and courage among his peers, reminding us that even the youngest among us can inspire change. Baji's legacy serves as a powerful example of how personal sacrifice in the face of adversity can lead to a greater sense of purpose and inspire future generations.

In conclusion, life's events—both challenging and transformative—offer us invaluable lessons if we take the time to reflect and learn from them. Whether it's embracing change like Sunil Gavaskar, drawing insights from failures such as ISRO's Chandrayaan missions, cultivating resilience exemplified by Abraham Lincoln, or finding purpose in adversity as shown by Baji Rout, each experience contributes to our growth. By recognizing the positive impacts of our past, we empower ourselves to navigate the present and future with confidence, turning every moment into an opportunity for personal development and meaningful change.

71

Unlocking the Power of the Mind

Conviction and the Human Potential

PSTO-71: Mind moves at high speed, even much beyond the speed of light. Yet, we encounter people who can drive their mind with much élan. It's time that we realize that we also can do it. We do not have to be a super-human to be able to do it. Probably, we just have to be convinced ourselves that we can do it!

The human mind is a remarkable force that can move at speeds beyond imagination. Yet, we often encounter individuals who seem to harness their minds with exceptional finesse. It's time we recognize that we, too, can tap into this potential. This chapter explores the idea that we don't need to be superhuman to achieve extraordinary mental feats; we just need to believe in our capacity to do so. Real-life examples demonstrate the transformative power of conviction and the untapped potential of the human mind.

1. The Inner Power of Conviction

The mind is a powerful instrument, but it requires conviction to unlock its potential. The inner power of conviction is embodied by Steven Gerrard, the legendary Liverpool captain. Throughout his career, Gerrard displayed an unshakeable belief in his ability to lead and inspire his team, even in the most challenging moments. One of the finest examples of his conviction was the 2005 Champions League final, where Liverpool trailed 3-0 at halftime. Gerrard's unwavering belief in a comeback fuelled his team's historic turnaround to win the title. His conviction, both in himself and his team, shows how inner strength can drive resilience and achieve the extraordinary.

2. Training the Mind for Excellence

The mind can be trained for excellence through deliberate practice and belief. Roger Federer, the tennis legend, has not only mastered the physical aspects of the game but also honed his mental acumen. His unwavering belief in his abilities has allowed him to achieve unparalleled success in the sport.

3. The Resilience of Human Potential

Human potential is often underestimated. The resilience of human potential is powerfully illustrated by Bhima Bhoi, the blind poet and saint from Odisha. Despite losing his sight, Bhima Bhoi's inner vision remained clear, and he used his poetic voice to advocate for justice, compassion, and equality. His profound spiritual writings, rooted in the Mahima Dharma, continue to inspire generations. Bhima Bhoi's resilience in overcoming his physical limitations to convey powerful messages of social change and human dignity demonstrates the boundless potential of the human spirit to rise above adversity and leave a lasting impact.

4. Precision Mindset

Jonny Wilkinson, the English rugby union legend, is known for his remarkable ability to stay mentally focused during high-pressure moments, such as his famous drop goal in the 2003 Rugby World Cup final. He has spoken extensively about how he trained his mind to stay in control during intense moments, focusing on precision and clarity rather than letting the chaos of the game overwhelm him. His mental discipline shows that anyone can achieve a high level of mind control with practice and belief.

The potential of the human mind is vast, and unlocking it begins with conviction. The stories of Steven Gerrard, Roger Federer, Bhima Bhoi, and Johny Wilkinson highlight that exceptional mental feats are not reserved for superhumans. They are achievable through belief in one's abilities and deliberate practice. It is a reminder that the human mind is a boundless resource waiting to be tapped. By recognizing our own capacity for greatness and nurturing our conviction, we can move beyond the limits we've placed on ourselves. The mind's speed and power are ours to harness, not as a superhuman ability but as a testament to the incredible potential inherent in every individual.

72

The Untapped Potential of Ideas

Nurturing Gems in the Making

PSTO-72: How often do we shut down an idea, even before it's described to us? Ideas, however trivial it may sound or appear to us in the first instance, may turn out to be a gem, when listened to, acted upon and encouraged by someone. Can that someone be us? We may decide.

Often, we dismiss ideas prematurely, failing to recognize their potential. However trivial they may seem at first glance, ideas can transform into precious gems when given a chance, nurtured, and encouraged. This chapter explores the importance of being open to ideas, regardless of their initial appearance, and emphasizes the role we can play in fostering innovation and creativity. Real-life examples illustrate the transformative power of this perspective.

1. The Hidden Value of Everyday Ideas

Everyday ideas can hold hidden value. Take the example of the Post-it note, a simple concept that originated from a failed adhesive experiment. It was only when someone recognized its potential and encouraged its development that this everyday idea became a revolutionary product.

2. Empowering Creativity in the Workplace

A culture of idea encouragement can drive innovation. Google's "20% time" policy allows employees to dedicate a portion of their workweek to pursuing personal projects and ideas. This culture has resulted in the development of many successful Google products, including Gmail.

3. Human-AI Collaboration

Chess grandmaster Garry Kasparov didn't dismiss the idea of using AI in chess, even when the concept was met with resistance by many traditionalists. He saw potential in human-AI collaboration, even after losing to IBM's Deep Blue in 1997. Rather than shutting down the idea, Kasparov explored how AI could complement human intellect. His open-minded approach allowed him to remain an influential figure in chess, and he became a proponent of human-machine symbiosis in other fields as well.

4. Innovation: Concept of "Moneyball"

Billy Beane, a former baseball player and general manager of the Oakland A's, was initially met with skepticism when he proposed using data analytics to scout undervalued players—an idea that many in Major League Baseball thought was too unconventional. However, Beane persisted, and his 'Moneyball' approach revolutionized how teams evaluated talent. By embracing a seemingly trivial idea and acting upon it, he changed the face of professional baseball and became an icon of innovative thinking.

5. Fostering Creativity in Education

Encouraging creativity and innovation in education is vital. Sir Ken Robinson, a leading expert on education and creativity, emphasized the need for educational systems to nurture rather than stifle students' creative potential. His advocacy has influenced educational reforms worldwide.

The untapped potential of ideas is a treasure trove waiting to be discovered. The stories of the Post-it note, Google's 20% time policy, Gary Kasparov, Billy Beane and Sir Ken Robinson illustrate the transformative power of nurturing and encouraging ideas, regardless of their initial appearance. It is a reminder that innovation and creativity flourish when ideas are given a chance to grow and evolve. The responsibility of being that someone who listens, acts upon, and encourages ideas can be ours to embrace. By doing so, we not only foster innovation but also create an environment where the gems of ideas, however humble they may seem, have the opportunity to shine and make a lasting impact on the world.

73

The Power of Compassion

Treating Every Human Being as Equal

PSTO-73: However powerful we may be, in terms of our position or authority, it does not give us any special privilege to hurt feelings of another human being. Rather, Power commands us to treat everyone as equal. We need to be conscious of it at every point of time.

Power, regardless of its magnitude, should never grant us the privilege to hurt the feelings of another human being. On the contrary, it commands us to treat every individual with respect and equality. This chapter explores the fundamental principle that power should be a force for compassion and justice. Real-life examples highlight the importance of conscious and compassionate leadership.

1. Power as a Force for Good

Power carries the responsibility to uplift, not to oppress. Lal Bahadur Shastri, the second Prime Minister of India, exemplified the transformative power of humility and integrity. His leadership during the Indo-Pakistani War of 1965 showcased his commitment to national unity and peace. Shastri famously coined the slogan "Jai Jawan Jai Kisan," emphasizing the importance of both soldiers and farmers in nation-building. By prioritizing cooperation and compassion over division, Shastri helped steer India towards progress, illustrating how true power can uplift a nation and its people.

2. The Role of Empathy in Leadership

Empathetic leadership recognizes the importance of every individual's feelings. Jacinda Ardern, the Prime Minister of New Zealand, exemplified this during her response to the Christchurch Mosque shootings. Her compassionate and inclusive approach not only provided comfort to the affected communities but also united the nation in mourning and solidarity. Ardern's ability to connect with people's emotions and demonstrate vulnerability in her leadership highlighted the power of empathy in positions of authority, showing that understanding and compassion can inspire resilience and healing in times of tragedy.

3. Respecting Diverse Perspectives

Power must respect diverse perspectives and voices. Ruth Bader Ginsburg, a U.S. Supreme Court Justice, championed gender equality and civil rights throughout her career. Her unwavering commitment to justice and equality is a testament to the power of inclusive and empathetic leadership.

4. Everyday Acts of Compassion

Compassion should extend to everyday interactions. Raja Harishchandra, a revered figure in Indian mythology, exemplified this principle through his unwavering commitment to truth and justice. Known for his immense compassion, he faced tremendous trials to uphold his principles, even sacrificing his kingdom and family. His story teaches the importance of empathy and selflessness, demonstrating that acts of compassion—regardless of the circumstances—can profoundly impact lives. Harishchandra's legacy inspires us to embody kindness and integrity in our daily interactions, reminding us that true compassion can shape a better world.

Power should never be a tool for hurting or oppressing others; it should be a force for compassion, justice, and equality. The stories of Lal Bhadur Shastri, Jacinda Ardern, Ruth Bader Ginsburg, and Raja Harischandra demonstrate that power can be a source of positive change when wielded with empathy and a commitment to the well-being of all. It is a reminder that regardless of our position or authority, we should consciously strive to treat every human being as equal and worthy of respect. Compassion is the true measure of power, and it is incumbent upon those in positions of influence to lead with empathy, inclusivity, and a commitment to the dignity and feelings of every individual. By doing so, we not only honour the principles of justice and equality but also create a more compassionate and just world for all.

74

Cultivating Relationships
A Lifelong Commitment

PSTO-74: Nurturing relationship is a full-time job. We have to keep on working on it. A few negligence, in terms of our action or words or gesture, may spoil it. We must remain aware of it.

Nurturing relationships is a continuous endeavour, demanding our unwavering attention and effort. Even a momentary lapse in our actions, words, or gestures can impact a relationship negatively. This chapter explores the idea that maintaining healthy relationships is a lifelong commitment that requires constant awareness and dedication. Real-life examples underscore the importance of this continuous effort.

1. The Fragility of Trust

Trust is the cornerstone of any healthy relationship. Mohammad Azharuddin, the former Indian cricket captain, experienced a significant erosion of trust when he was implicated in a match-fixing scandal. This betrayal not only tarnished his reputation but also damaged his relationships with teammates, fans, and the cricketing community. Azharuddin's fall from grace serves as a powerful reminder of how fragile trust can be and how quickly it can be lost, emphasizing the need for integrity in all aspects of life.

2. Communication and Understanding

Effective communication is key to maintaining healthy relationships, both personal and professional. When communication breaks down, the consequences can be profound and far-reaching. A poignant example is the tragedy of the Titanic. Despite being equipped with advanced technology for its time, critical warnings about icebergs went unheeded due to miscommunication and a lack of clarity among the crew. This failure to effectively communicate crucial information ultimately led to the ship's sinking and the loss of over 1,500 lives. The Titanic disaster serves as a stark reminder of the importance of clear and open communication, highlighting that misunderstandings can have catastrophic results and underscoring the need for vigilance and attentiveness in conveying vital information.

3. Forging Lasting Friendships

Friendships require ongoing effort and understanding. Mark Zuckerberg and Eduardo Saverin, co-founders of Facebook, experienced a falling out that strained their friendship. It serves as a reminder that even in the pursuit of success, maintaining personal relationships is essential.

4. Family Bonds

Family relationships require constant care. The strained relationship between Prince William and Prince Harry garnered public attention. Their journey to mend their bond highlights the ongoing work needed to nurture family relationships.

Nurturing relationships is a lifelong commitment that necessitates consistent effort, awareness, and care. The examples of Mohammad Azharuddin, the Titanic tragedy, Mark Zuckerberg and Eduardo Saverin & Princes of England underscore the importance of maintaining trust, communication, understanding, and forgiveness in relationships. It is a reminder that, irrespective of the type of relationship, no effort is too small when it comes to preserving the bonds that enrich our lives. By remaining aware of the fragility of relationships and actively working to nurture them, we can build and sustain meaningful connections that stand the test of time. Relationships, like gardens, flourish when tended to regularly, and they reward us with the beauty of lasting connections and shared experiences.

75

Rising Above Blame

A Deeper Look into Life's Challenges

PSTO-75: Many a times, when we feel let down, more often than not our immediate reaction is to assign the cause to a person. However, most of the time, we find ourselves not to be correct in this assessment of ours. Rather, I feel we must look into the events leading to this. I am sure we will find more than hundred ways to improve the situation and improve ourselves too.

In moments of disappointment or frustration, our instinct is often to assign blame to a person. However, more often than not, this assessment falls short of capturing the complexities of the situation. This chapter explores the idea that, instead of hastily assigning blame, we should examine the events leading to our challenges. By doing so, we can discover numerous ways to improve not only the situation but also ourselves. Real-life examples illustrate the wisdom of this approach.

1. The Reflex of Blame

Blaming others is a natural reaction when things go wrong. Consider the story of the "Challenger" space shuttle disaster. Initially, the blame was placed on the engineers, but a closer examination revealed systemic issues within NASA's decision-making processes.

2. Examining Root Causes

True solutions come from understanding root causes. The 2008 financial crisis is an example. While individuals were blamed for reckless behavior, the crisis had deeper systemic issues, including regulatory failures and unsustainable lending practices.

3. Personal Growth Through Self-Reflection

Self-reflection is a powerful tool for personal growth, allowing individuals to learn from their experiences and make meaningful changes in their lives. A great example of this is Swami Vivekananda, whose journey was marked by deep introspection and self-discovery. Before becoming a renowned spiritual leader, Vivekananda faced numerous challenges and uncertainties, including questions about his purpose and beliefs. Instead of succumbing to doubt, he engaged in self-reflection, exploring various philosophies and practices to understand his own identity and mission. This process of introspection not only strengthened his resolve but also led him to articulate a vision of spirituality that emphasized the importance of self-awareness and service to humanity. Vivekananda's commitment to personal growth through self-reflection ultimately allowed him to inspire millions and contribute significantly to the revival of Hindu philosophy. His life illustrates how taking the time to reflect can transform challenges into opportunities for growth and lead to profound impacts on both oneself and the wider world.

4. Conflict Resolution and Empathy

In personal relationships, blaming can hinder resolution. The Israeli-Palestinian conflict is a complex example where both sides have assigned blame for decades. Progress toward peace requires empathy and a deeper understanding of each other's perspectives.

Assigning blame may provide temporary relief, but it rarely leads to lasting solutions. The stories of the "Challenger" disaster, the 2008 financial crisis, Swami Vivekananda and the Israeli-Palestinian conflict demonstrate the power of looking beyond blame to identify root causes and find meaningful solutions. By examining the events leading to our challenges, we not only improve the situation but also embark on a journey of personal growth and self-improvement. It is a reminder that life's challenges are opportunities for learning and growth. Instead of assigning blame, we can choose to adopt a problem-solving mindset, fostering a more constructive and fulfilling path forward for ourselves and those around us.

76

Innovation

Reaching the Destination in the Most Productive Way?

PSTO-76: Is innovation nothing but reaching the same destination in the most productive way? Leaders need to ponder over it and guide their teams accordingly.

Innovation, at its core, is about finding the most productive and efficient path to a destination. Leaders, tasked with guiding their teams to success, should ponder this concept carefully. This essay explores the idea that innovation is not always about reinventing the wheel but often about optimizing existing processes to reach the same destination more effectively. Real-life examples illustrate the significance of this perspective.

1. Optimizing Efficiency Through Innovation

Efficiency is a hallmark of innovation. Henry Ford's assembly line revolutionized the automotive industry by streamlining production processes, making cars more affordable and accessible to the masses. His innovation was about reaching the destination of automobile manufacturing more productively.

2. Technology as a Productivity Booster

Technology plays a significant role in innovation. Apple's introduction of the iPhone transformed the way we communicate and access information. While the destination (communication) remained the same, the iPhone made the journey more productive and convenient.

3. Sustainable Innovation

Sustainability is a critical aspect of modern innovation. Companies like Tesla are focused on reaching the destination of clean energy and transportation more sustainably. Their electric vehicles and renewable energy solutions represent innovative ways to achieve this goal.

4. Process Optimization in Business

Business leaders constantly seek ways to optimize processes. Amazon's development of an efficient supply chain and distribution network is an example. Their innovation lies in reaching the destination of delivering products to customers more quickly and cost-effectively.

5. Innovation in Healthcare

Healthcare innovation often revolves around improving patient outcomes and reducing costs. Telemedicine platforms like Teladoc provide a more productive way to reach the destination of healthcare access, allowing patients to connect with doctors remotely.

Innovation is not always about creating something entirely new; it can be about optimizing existing processes to reach the same destination more efficiently and productively. The examples of Henry Ford, Apple, Tesla, Amazon, and Teladoc demonstrate that innovation often revolves around making the journey more convenient, sustainable, or cost-effective. Leaders should recognize that innovation is a powerful tool for achieving organizational goals and guiding their teams to success. By encouraging a culture of innovation that values efficiency and continuous improvement, leaders can help their organizations reach their destinations more effectively and remain competitive in a rapidly evolving world. Ultimately, innovation is about finding better, more productive ways to achieve the desired outcome, and it should be a cornerstone of leadership in the modern era.

77

Harnessing Inspiration

The Art of Discovery and Transformation

PSTO-77: Inspirations comes from all quarters. It's on us as to how we detect, assimilate and take advantage of it.

Inspiration has the remarkable ability to emerge from unexpected sources and moments. However, its true power lies in how we recognize, absorb, and leverage it. This chapter delves into the idea that inspiration is all around us, waiting to be discovered and harnessed. Real-life examples demonstrate the transformative potential of recognizing and acting upon inspiration.

1. Inspiration from Daily Struggles

Anand Kumar, the founder of the Super 30 program, found inspiration in the struggles of underprivileged students. Coming from a modest background himself, he saw how poverty limited talented students' access to quality education. Inspired by their determination, he started the Super 30 initiative, providing free coaching to underprivileged students for IIT entrance exams. Anand's ability to detect inspiration from the everyday challenges of the people around him enabled him to make a significant impact on the lives of aspiring engineers from economically disadvantaged backgrounds.

2. Embracing Diverse Perspectives

Inspiration flourishes when we embrace diverse perspectives. The civil rights movement in the United States drew inspiration from Mahatma Gandhi's nonviolent resistance. Martin Luther King Jr. applied Gandhi's principles to advance the cause of civil rights and social justice.

3. Nature as a Source of Insight

Nature is a wellspring of inspiration, providing valuable insights that can lead to groundbreaking innovations. A striking example is Christopher Columbus, whose voyages were deeply influenced by observations of the natural world. Driven by a desire to find a new trade route to Asia, Columbus closely studied the stars, ocean currents, and wind patterns to navigate the uncharted waters of the Atlantic. His keen observations of the natural environment not only informed his navigation techniques but also helped him understand the behaviors of the sea and the skies, which were crucial for long-distance travel. Columbus's journey, although controversial, opened the door to the Age of Exploration and profoundly changed the course of history. By harnessing the knowledge and cues from nature, he was able to embark on a voyage that led to the discovery of the Americas. This illustrates how looking to nature for inspiration can guide innovation and exploration, revealing pathways that transform human understanding and connection to the world.

4. Everyday Moments of Epiphany

Everyday life can provide profound moments of inspiration. Archimedes, the ancient Greek mathematician, famously had a

"Eureka!" moment while taking a bath. He discovered the principle of displacement, which became fundamental in the study of volume and density.

Inspiration is an omnipresent force, waiting to be discovered and embraced. The examples of Anand Kumar, Martin Luther King Jr., Columbus, and Archimedes underscore the transformative potential of recognizing and acting upon inspiration. It is a reminder that inspiration is not limited to a select few; it is accessible to anyone willing to observe, interact, embrace diverse perspectives, and stay open to everyday moments of epiphany. By harnessing inspiration, we can catalyze innovation, ignite creativity, and drive positive change in our lives and the world. It is an invitation to cultivate a mindset that actively seeks and seizes the inspiration that surrounds us, for it is through these sparks of insight that we can illuminate new pathways to discovery and transformation.

78

Small Acts, Big Impact

The Power of Giving Back

PSTO-78: As human beings, it's natural to be in our thoughts to give back. But most of the times we wonder how we can. To me, it may not be a big intervention to start with. Can we just begin by planting a tree or by keeping water for the birds and animals? Just a point to ponder.

The innate desire to give back is a universal human trait. Often, we wonder how we can make a difference, and the answer can be surprisingly simple. Small acts of kindness, such as planting a tree or providing water for birds and animals, can have a significant and lasting impact. This chapter explores the idea that even the smallest gestures can initiate positive change in the world. Real-life examples illustrate the profound effect of these seemingly modest actions.

1. The Beauty of Planting Trees

Planting a tree may seem like a small act, but it holds the power to transform landscapes and lives. A shining example of this is Thimmakka, often referred to as the "Tree Woman of India." Despite facing poverty and personal challenges, she and her husband began planting banyan trees along a barren stretch of road in Karnataka, determined to make a difference. Over the years, they planted and nurtured 385 banyan trees, creating a green canopy that has become a symbol of environmental stewardship. Thimmakka's dedication proves that even humble efforts can leave a profound, lasting impact on the environment. Her story inspires us to recognize that small acts of caring for nature, can grow into legacies that benefit generations to come.

2. Nourishing Life with Water

Providing water for birds and animals may seem like a simple gesture, yet it holds the potential to nurture entire ecosystems. Take the example of Jadav Payeng, famously known as the "Forest Man of India." Payeng started by planting trees and digging ponds on a barren island in the Brahmaputra River, aiming to create a haven for wildlife. Over the years, his dedication led to the birth of a thriving forest teeming with biodiversity. What began as small, consistent acts of compassion for nature evolved into a lush ecosystem that supports countless species today. His efforts remind us that even small actions, when sustained over time, can lead to monumental change.

3. Feeding the Hungry

Addressing hunger often starts with a simple gesture, such as offering a meal. Mary McLeod Bethune, an iconic educator and civil rights leader, understood this deeply. During the Great Depression, she began a modest soup kitchen in her community to provide food for those in need. Though it started small, her efforts quickly expanded, helping to feed hundreds of struggling families. Her initiative showed that the impact of giving back, especially in times of crisis, can grow beyond imagination, providing not only sustenance but also hope to those facing adversity.

4. Acts of Kindness

Small acts of kindness, though often overlooked, can make a significant difference in someone's life. A story that captures this idea is one involving Tom Hanks, the beloved actor known not only for his performances but also for his genuine humanity. During a visit to New York City, Hanks found a cab driver's lost ID card and went out of his way to return it. This simple act of honesty and kindness not only helped the driver recover an important possession but also sparked a chain of goodwill. It's a reminder that kindness, no matter how small, can spread positivity far beyond its initial impact.

The desire to give back need not be daunting or grandiose; it can begin with the simplest of gestures. The stories of Thimmakka, Jadav Payeng, Mary McLeod Bethune, and Tom Hanks highlight the profound impact of small acts of kindness and generosity. It is a reminder that every individual has the power to make a difference, no matter how modest their means or actions. By starting with these small, meaningful steps, we not only create positive change in the world but also inspire others to join in. These small acts, collectively, form a tapestry of compassion and goodwill that can transform communities, uplift lives, and make the world a better place for all. It's a point to ponder and an invitation to embrace the potential for positive change that lies within each of us.

79

The Golden Rule of Respect

Acknowledging Others' Expertise

PSTO-79: Don't we feel a sense of repulse when we are asked to do something which we are sure may not be the right for the occasion. Yet how often do we do the same to others without realising that the person being asked may know the path or solution much better? Yes, we do need to be conscious about it, all the time.

It's natural to feel a sense of discomfort when asked to do something we believe is not the right solution for a situation. However, we must reflect on how often we impose our own solutions on others without recognizing their expertise. This chapter explores the importance of being conscious about respecting others' knowledge and experiences. Real-life examples illustrate the value of acknowledging and valuing the insights and capabilities of others.

1. The Weight of Unwanted Solutions

Being asked to implement a solution that doesn't align with expertise can be not only frustrating but also dangerous. The tragic story of the Challenger space shuttle disaster in 1986 is a powerful example of this. Engineers had voiced their concerns about the faulty O-rings in freezing temperatures, warning that the shuttle wasn't safe to launch. However, their expertise was dismissed by management, who prioritized schedule and external pressures over technical advice. The result was catastrophic. This tragedy illustrates the critical importance of respecting specialized knowledge. It is a stark reminder that when expertise is sidelined, the price can be unimaginably high.

2. Consulting the Local Experts

In the field of international development, acknowledging local expertise is crucial for creating sustainable solutions. The PlayPump water system, initially seen as an innovative way to provide clean water to rural African communities, ultimately failed because it did not consider the input of local experts. The system, which required children to pump water by playing on a merry-go-round, quickly became impractical as it did not meet the community's needs and demands. Local residents and engineers, who had more intimate knowledge of the area's water requirements, were not sufficiently consulted. This failure highlights the importance of listening to those who best understand the unique challenges of their environments.

3. Listening to Healthcare Professionals

In healthcare, respecting the expertise of medical professionals is not only wise but can be life-saving. Dr. Ignaz Semmelweis, a 19th-century physician, discovered that handwashing drastically reduced the spread of infections in hospitals. Despite presenting clear evidence, his advice was initially dismissed by his peers, resulting in preventable deaths. It took years for his insights to gain the recognition they deserved, but his persistence eventually led to the adoption of hand hygiene practices that are now fundamental to healthcare worldwide.

4. Respecting Individual Autonomy

In personal relationships, respecting each other's autonomy and expertise is equally important. Amal and George Clooney's partnership exemplifies this. While George is a globally recognized actor, Amal is a renowned human rights lawyer with a distinguished career of her own. Rather than allowing his fame to overshadow her achievements, George openly acknowledges and celebrates Amal's expertise in her field. Their relationship is a testament to the idea that mutual respect for one another's knowledge and career paths strengthens personal bonds.

The discomfort of being asked to implement an unsuitable solution should remind us to be conscious of how we treat others. The examples of the Challenger disaster, the Play Pump failure, Dr. Ignaz Semmelweis, and Amal and George Clooney underscore the importance of acknowledging and respecting others' expertise. It is a reminder that we should actively seek and value the insights and capabilities of those around us. By doing so, we not only promote innovation and success but also foster a culture of respect and collaboration. It is an invitation to be conscious of our actions and choices, recognizing that, just as we desire respect for our expertise, others deserve the same consideration and appreciation for their knowledge and experiences.

80

Embracing Authenticity
The Path to Being Yourself

PSTO-80: Be yourself at all points of time. Does it help? To me, yes it does. As you don't have to recreate. Is it easy? Again to me, it's not. But it is doable. We can start doing it from today.

The idea of being yourself at all times is a powerful one, but it isn't always easy to achieve. Yet, it offers numerous benefits, as it eliminates the need to recreate or wear masks. This chapter explores the value of authenticity and the journey to being oneself. Real-life examples illustrate the transformative impact of embracing and celebrating one's true self.

1. The Struggle to Be Authentic

Being true to oneself can be an uphill battle, especially when societal norms dictate otherwise. Pat Cummins, the current captain of the Australian cricket team, exemplifies the struggle to be authentic in a world where tradition and expectation can stifle individuality. Historically, Australian cricket captains have been known for their aggressive, hard-nosed leadership styles, with an emphasis on toughness and winning at all costs. Cummins, however, faced the challenge of staying true to his own values in a culture that prized aggression over empathy. Rather than conforming, he embraced a leadership approach based on openness, empathy, and respect. He advocated for mental health awareness, environmental sustainability, and inclusivity—issues not traditionally associated with cricket leadership. By standing firm in his beliefs, even when they clashed with the past image of an Australian captain, Cummins redefined what it means to lead.

2. Unleashing Creativity

Authenticity is a gateway to unleashing creativity, allowing individuals to express their true selves through their work. Michelangelo, the legendary Renaissance artist, exemplified this through his art. His masterpieces, such as the Sistine Chapel ceiling and the statue of David, reveal not only technical brilliance but also his deep connection to his inner self. Michelangelo's commitment to his artistic vision was unwavering, even in the face of criticism and challenges. He was known for defying conventions of his time, rejecting easy commissions in favor of projects that allowed him to explore the depths of human emotion and spirituality. By embracing his authentic voice and refusing to compromise on his ideals, Michelangelo's work transcended mere craftsmanship to become timeless expressions of the human experience.

3. Staying True to Herself

P.V. Sindhu, India's badminton sensation, has consistently stayed true to her identity and playing style despite global pressure to conform. She has openly spoken about the challenges of staying authentic in a competitive environment but emphasizes that her success comes from remaining herself on and off the court. This approach helped her achieve great success, including multiple world titles and Olympic medals, showing that being oneself is both difficult and rewarding.

Being yourself at all times may not be easy, but it is a journey worth embarking on. The examples of Pat Cummins, Michelangelo, and P. V. Sindhu illustrate the transformative power of authenticity. It is a reminder that authenticity is not only liberating but also a catalyst for creativity, trust, and meaningful relationships. By embracing and celebrating our true selves, we not only find inner peace but also inspire others to do the same. The journey to authenticity may have challenges, but it begins with the decision to be ourselves, starting from today. It is an invitation to recognize that the most genuine version of ourselves is the one that can make the greatest impact on the world and leave a lasting legacy of authenticity for generations to come.

81

The Power of Perspective

Elevating Every Role to Significance

PSTO-81: When I was young, one of my seniors used to tell me; "You give me any job, I will strive to make it the most important one in the Organisation". I used to wonder if it's practically feasible. When I look at it now, I strongly feel it's possible. It's on us to make it happen. Quite intriguing! Is it or Isn't it?

The idea that any job can be made the most important one in an organization might seem intriguing at first glance. However, it is entirely feasible, and it underscores the profound impact of perspective. This chapter delves into the concept of elevating every role to significance and how it is within our power to make it happen. Real-life examples demonstrate the transformative potential of this approach.

1. Inspiring a Culture of Excellence

Recognizing the value of every role within an organization can inspire a culture of excellence, where each individual feels empowered to contribute their best. A prime example is Zappos, the online shoe and clothing retailer famous for its dedication to customer service. At Zappos, employees are not merely fulfilling routine tasks; even call center staff are given the autonomy and trust to go beyond standard procedures to delight customers. Whether it's offering personalized service or going the extra mile to resolve an issue, these employees understand the significance of their roles. By fostering a perspective where each interaction is viewed as an opportunity to make a meaningful impact, Zappos has cultivated an environment where excellence thrives across all levels of the organization.

2. The Unsung Heroes

Behind every success story are the often-overlooked individuals whose contributions are critical but not always recognized. Janitors, for instance, perform the essential work of maintaining clean, safe, and functional environments, yet their role is rarely celebrated. During World War II, the iconic figure of Rosie the Riveter emerged as a symbol of the millions of women who took on manufacturing jobs in factories while men were off at war. These women, many of whom had never worked in such roles before, produced planes, ships, and ammunition that were crucial to the war effort. Though their contributions were essential to the nation's success, their recognition was minimal at the time. Rosie the Riveter represents the countless unsung heroes whose work, though often unseen, elevates the success of the whole.

3. Transforming Perceptions

Coco Chanel, a legendary fashion designer, revolutionized women's fashion by turning every aspect of her work into a statement of importance. Whether designing a dress or creating a marketing campaign, Chanel approached each task with the belief that it could redefine the industry. Her relentless pursuit of excellence in every job she undertook shows that it is possible to elevate any responsibility to a position of significance through passion and commitment.

Elevating every role to significance is not only possible but also a transformative approach that can enrich organizations and societies. The examples of Zappos, Rosie the Riveter, and Coco Chanel highlight the power of perspective and inclusivity. It is a reminder that every role, no matter how seemingly small, contributes to the collective success of an organization or a cause. By recognizing and celebrating the significance of each role, we inspire excellence, empower individuals, and create a culture where everyone feels valued and motivated to excel. It is a perspective that challenges us to view the world through a different lens—one that reveals the potential for greatness in every role, task, and individual.

82

Staying True to Yourself

Navigating the Diverse Opinions on Your Journey

PSTO-82: In our journey of life, we come across varieties of people. While a of them may like us or our work, others may not. But that should never deter us from doing what we are engaged in as long as it has the approval of our conscience.

Life's journey introduces us to a wide array of people, each with their own opinions and perspectives. Some may appreciate us and our work, while others may not share the same enthusiasm. However, it is crucial to remain steadfast in our pursuits as long as our actions align with our conscience. This chapter explores the importance of staying true to oneself in the face of diverse opinions and offers real-life examples to illustrate this principle.

1. The Art of Creativity

For creative individuals, staying true to their vision often means navigating through waves of resistance, criticism, and doubt from others. Vincent van Gogh, now celebrated as one of the greatest artists in history, epitomized this struggle. During his lifetime, van Gogh faced relentless rejection, with his work being dismissed by critics and ignored by the public. His bold use of color, emotive brushstrokes, and unconventional style were seen as out of step with the artistic norms of the time. Despite these harsh opinions, van Gogh refused to abandon his passion and artistic vision. He remained committed to expressing his inner world, often channeling his emotional intensity into masterpieces like Starry Night and Sunflowers.

2. Championing Social Justice

Staying true to one's principles in the pursuit of social justice often means challenging the status quo and enduring opposition. Vinoba Bhave, a spiritual leader and social reformer, exemplified this commitment in his lifelong work for equality and justice. As the founder of the Bhoodan (land gift) movement, Bhave aimed to address India's deep-rooted issue of land inequality. His vision was simple yet radical: persuade wealthy landowners to voluntarily donate land to the landless poor. Bhave faced significant skepticism from many who doubted the feasibility of his mission. Yet, he remained unwavering in his belief that moral persuasion and nonviolent means could bring about transformative change. Walking thousands of miles across rural India, Bhave spoke to landowners and peasants alike, convincing them of the ethical imperative of sharing their land. His relentless dedication resulted in millions of acres being redistributed.

3. Staying True to Purpose

Remaining focused on one's purpose, especially in the face of challenges and opposition, is key to achieving extraordinary outcomes. Dr. Vikram Sarabhai, often referred to as the father of India's space program, exemplified this principle. When Sarabhai first proposed the idea of establishing a space research program in India, the nation was still grappling with poverty and the aftereffects of colonialism. Critics questioned the need for such an ambitious project, arguing that India's resources should be focused on basic development rather than scientific exploration. Despite the criticism and doubts, Sarabhai remained true to his vision of using space technology for national development. He firmly believed that space exploration could serve practical purposes, such as improving communication, weather forecasting, and natural resource management, thereby uplifting the country's socio-economic landscape. His persistence led to the founding of the Indian Space Research Organisation (ISRO), which has since become one of the world's leading space agencies.

Encountering diverse opinions and criticism is an inherent part of life's journey. The examples of Vincent van Gogh, Vinoba Bhave, and Dr. Vikram Sarabhai underscore the importance of staying true to oneself and one's principles, even in the face of adversity and opposition. It is a reminder that, as long as our actions align with our conscience and our sense of purpose, external opinions should not deter us. By remaining steadfast in our pursuits, we not only honor our authentic selves but also contribute to positive change and progress in the world. It is an invitation to navigate life's journey with resilience and unwavering commitment to our beliefs and convictions, knowing that staying true to ourselves is the surest path to personal fulfilment and making a meaningful impact on others and society.

83

Gift of Being-Human

Making Our Lives Count Through Acts of Kindness

PSTO-83: We are truly blessed to have been born as humans. We must then make it count for us as well as others through our deeds. There may be a number of ways of doing so. Can we begin by just extending a helping hand to people around us? Just a point to ponder.

The gift of human life is a profound blessing. It calls us to make our existence meaningful, not just for ourselves but also for others. There are countless ways to achieve this, but perhaps one of the most accessible is by extending a helping hand to those around us. This chapter explores the notion that acts of kindness are a simple yet powerful means of making our lives count. Real-life examples demonstrate the transformative impact of reaching out to others with compassion and empathy.

1. Supporting the Vulnerable

Acts of kindness often take the form of supporting the most vulnerable in society. The Wadata Talaka Safety Net program in Niger is a striking example of how compassion can transform lives.

This initiative provides financial assistance and resources to the poorest households, enabling them to meet basic needs like food, healthcare, and education. In a country where poverty is widespread, the program goes beyond simple charity by fostering dignity and self-reliance. By helping families regain their footing, the Wadata Talaka program not only offers a lifeline to individuals in dire need but also strengthens the social fabric of entire communities.

2. Empathy in Action

Empathy is a uniquely human trait that compels us to help others, often in extraordinary ways. The story of a firefighter carrying a young girl to safety during the Oklahoma City bombing is a moving example of empathy in action. In the midst of chaos and devastation, the firefighter's immediate response was not just to do his job but to save lives, putting himself at risk for the sake of others. His act of bravery, driven by an innate sense of compassion, exemplifies how empathy can turn ordinary individuals into heroes in moments of crisis. Through his selflessness, he not only saved the girl's life but also offered hope in a time of overwhelming despair.

3. Creating Communities of Kindness

Kindness has the ability to bring people together and create communities rooted in compassion. The "Little Free Library" movement is a shining example of how small acts of sharing can foster a sense of connection and generosity. What began as a simple idea—placing small book-sharing boxes in neighborhoods—has grown into a global initiative, with thousands of libraries popping up in communities around the world. By encouraging neighbors to share books with one another, these small libraries promote literacy and build a culture of kindness. They create spaces where people of all ages and backgrounds can come together, united by the shared joy of reading. This initiative shows how even the simplest acts, like sharing a book, can have a ripple effect, spreading kindness and fostering stronger, more engaged communities.

Being born as humans is a remarkable gift that calls us to make our lives count through our deeds. Acts of kindness, as demonstrated by the Wadata Talak Safety Net programme, the Oklahoma City firefighter, and the "Free Little Library" initiative, show that extending a helping hand is a simple yet profound way to fulfil this calling. These acts not only brighten the lives of those we touch but also create a ripple effect of positivity and compassion in the world. It is a reminder that, regardless of our circumstances or resources, we all have the capacity to make a difference through our actions. By embracing kindness and empathy as guiding principles, we can ensure that our lives truly count, leaving a legacy of love and goodwill for future generations to cherish and build upon.

84

From Storm to Sunshine
Embracing Life's Ebb and Flow

PSTO-84: There must have been many days in our lives when everything seemed to be going wrong. Does it not disturb us a lot at that point of time? But have we ever realised that it didn't last perennially. And when the clouds moved away, the new sunrays brought more shine in.

Life often presents us with days when everything seems to go wrong, casting a shadow over our spirits. In those moments, it's easy to feel disheartened. Yet, if we reflect on our journey, we realize that these storms don't last forever. Eventually, the clouds part, making way for the warming rays of sunshine. This chapter explores the idea that life's ebb and flow, with its ups and downs, is a natural rhythm that can bring greater brightness and resilience. Real-life incidents illustrate the transformative power of embracing life's fluctuations.

1. Navigating Personal Challenges

Dr. Manoj Kumar Sharma, an Indian Police Service (IPS) officer, exemplifies the strength required to navigate such obstacles. Dr.

Sharma faced significant adversities throughout his academic journey. Instead of allowing these to define him, he embraced the failure as a stepping stone to success. With unwavering determination, he worked tirelessly to overcome his academic challenges, ultimately succeeding in the civil services examination and earning his place as an IPS officer. His journey from failure to triumph not only highlights the importance of perseverance but also serves as an inspiring tale for countless students facing similar struggles. His life story became the basis for the film 12th Fail, which illustrates how embracing setbacks can lead to personal growth and achievement.

2. Enduring Difficult Times

Enduring difficult times can often reveal the strength of one's character, as demonstrated by Indian Prime Minister Narendra Modi. Modi faced numerous challenges throughout his political career, particularly during the early years when he was marginalized and faced criticism from various quarters. Despite these setbacks, he remained steadfast in his vision for India, emphasizing economic growth, social reform, and national pride. His ability to endure the storms of political opposition and public scrutiny eventually led to his emergence as a powerful leader. Modi's journey is a testament to the importance of resilience and determination; his unwavering focus on his goals allowed him to turn adversity into opportunity.

3. Embracing Health Challenges

Health challenges can profoundly impact one's life, yet they also present opportunities for growth and inspiration. Suhas Yathiraj, a Para Olympian and IAS officer, embodies this spirit of resilience. Born with a physical disability that could have limited his aspirations, Suhas chose to embrace his challenges instead. He not only excelled in sports, earning two silver medals in badminton in Paralympics, but also pursued a distinguished career in civil service, demonstrating that one's circumstances do not define their potential. Suhas's journey from facing societal stigma to becoming a role model for many showcases the power of determination and self-acceptance. His story inspires countless individuals facing their own health challenges to embrace their journey and strive for excellence.

Life's ebb and flow, with its storms and sunshine, is a natural and inevitable part of the human experience. The examples of Dr. Manoj Kumar Sharma, PM Modi and Suhas Yathiraj demonstrate the transformative power of embracing life's fluctuations. It is a reminder that challenges, setbacks, and difficult days are temporary. They can serve as catalysts for growth, resilience, and personal transformation. By weathering the storms with courage and tenacity, we can emerge from them stronger, wiser, and more appreciative of the brightness that follows. It is an invitation to embrace life's natural rhythm, recognizing that even in our darkest moments, the promise of sunshine and renewal is always on the horizon, ready to bring greater shine and resilience into our lives.

85

The Power of Response

Taking Control of Our Reactions

PSTO-85: Don't we all realise the reality that how we react to a situation, is completely dependent on us? Yet, how is it that normally we tend to put the onus on the circumstances or the personalities involved? It's time we realise it and work on it, consciously.

It's a reality we all recognize: how we react to a situation is entirely dependent on us. However, it's also true that we often attribute our reactions to external circumstances or the personalities involved. It's time to realize and consciously work on taking control of our responses. This chapter explores the significance of personal responsibility in our reactions, with real-life examples that illustrate the transformative power of intentional response.

1. Transforming Conflict Through Empathy

In conflict situations, the power of empathy can profoundly transform our reactions and outcomes. Daryl Davis, an African American musician, serves as a remarkable example of this principle in action. Rather than responding to the hostility and prejudice of the Ku Klux Klan with anger or aggression, Davis took a courageous approach by initiating dialogues with its members. He sought to understand their perspectives and shared his own experiences, fostering genuine conversations grounded in empathy and human connection. Through these heartfelt interactions, Davis was able to break down barriers of hatred and misinformation, successfully persuading numerous Klan members to leave the organization.

2. Turning Setbacks into Opportunities

Turning setbacks into opportunities requires resilience and a proactive mindset, as exemplified by Madhusudan Das, a prominent leader from Odisha. Growing up in a humble environment, Das faced numerous challenges. One notable childhood incident that has become part of Odisha's folklore illustrates his character. While walking to school one day, he fell on a poorly maintained road and, instead of simply getting up and continuing, he took it upon himself to repair the damaged section. This act of initiative not only showcased his resourcefulness but also reflected his belief that change begins with individual action. Madhusudan excelled academically, eventually becoming a successful lawyer and a champion for the rights of marginalized communities.

3. Personal Responsibility in Relationships

In the realm of personal relationships, our reactions hold significant power in shaping our interactions. Carl Rogers, a pioneering psychologist, underscored the vital role of empathy and active listening in fostering healthy relationships. Through his client-centred therapy approach, Rogers transformed the field of psychology by emphasizing the importance of understanding clients' feelings and perspectives. He believed that when individuals feel heard and validated, they are more likely to engage positively in the therapeutic process. Rogers' emphasis on personal responsibility in how we respond to others promotes a culture of openness and respect. By actively choosing to listen and empathize, we can cultivate deeper connections and navigate conflicts more effectively.

The power to control our reactions lies within us, and it is a reality we must acknowledge and embrace. The examples of Daryl Davis, Madhusudan Das, and Carl Rogers underscore the transformative potential of intentional response. It is a reminder that, regardless of external circumstances or the personalities involved, we possess the agency to choose our reactions. By taking personal responsibility for our responses, we can navigate life's challenges with grace, empathy, and resilience. It is an invitation to cultivate mindfulness, empathy, and positivity as guiding principles, recognizing that our reactions have the power to shape our experiences and the world around us. As we consciously work on this aspect of our lives, we become architects of our own inner peace and agents of positive change in our interactions with others.

86

The Morning Gratitude Ritual

Embracing the Gift of a New Day

PSTO-86: How many of us thank the Almighty the first thing in the morning? To the best of my knowledge, all religions, all beliefs teach us to do so. Yet, most of us tend to forget it. That fact that we have opened our eyes in the morning, is a precursor to the plan of Almighty having granted us some more time to enjoy the beauty of this world in company of our near and dear ones. It is, therefore, so prudent on our part to be eternally thankful.

In the rush of our daily lives, it's easy to forget the simplest yet most profound act of gratitude – thanking the Almighty for a new day. Across all religions and belief systems, this practice is deeply rooted. Yet, it often slips our minds. This chapter explores the importance of beginning our day with gratitude, acknowledging the precious gift of waking up to experience the world and share it with our loved ones and highlights its transformative power.

1. The Universal Practice of Gratitude

Gratitude is a universal practice that transcends religious and cultural boundaries, serving as a powerful reminder of the interconnectedness of humanity. Across the globe, people engage in morning rituals that express their thankfulness for a new day. For instance, Muslims begin their day with the Fajr prayer, a time dedicated to reflection and gratitude, acknowledging the blessings in their lives. Similarly, Christians may offer morning prayers, seeking guidance and expressing appreciation for their relationships and opportunities. Hindus practice mindfulness and Yoga in the morning, focusing on their breath and cultivating a sense of gratitude for the present moment. These diverse expressions of thankfulness highlight a shared human experience—recognizing the gift of life and the potential each day holds.

2. Strengthening Bonds with Loved Ones

Mornings offer a unique opportunity to cherish our relationships and express gratitude towards loved ones. The poignant wisdom imparted by Morrie Schwartz, as depicted in the book 'Tuesdays with Morrie', exemplifies this beautifully. Faced with a terminal illness, Morrie emphasized the significance of nurturing connections and expressing love daily. He encouraged those around him to prioritize meaningful interactions, reminding them that life's fleeting nature makes it all the more important to convey gratitude and affection. By starting the day with an acknowledgment of the people we hold dear—whether through a simple "thank you," a warm embrace, or heartfelt conversation—we can strengthen our bonds and create lasting memories.

3. The Healing Power of Gratitude

The healing power of gratitude is a profound concept, deeply rooted in various traditions and teachings, including Indic Wisdom. This ancient philosophy emphasizes the transformative effects of gratitude on the mind and spirit. By beginning each day with an attitude of thankfulness, individuals can cultivate a sense of inner peace and resilience. Indic teachings suggest that expressing gratitude shifts our focus from what we lack to what we have, fostering a positive mindset that can enhance our overall well-being. By embracing the gift of a new day with gratitude, we open ourselves to healing and personal growth, reinforcing the idea that our reactions to life's challenges can shape our experience of happiness and fulfilment.

Beginning our day with gratitude for the gift of a new morning is a universal practice deeply embedded in our beliefs and traditions. The examples from Religions and Cultures across the world including Indiac Wisdom and the case of Morrie Schwartz underscore the transformative power of this morning ritual. It is a reminder that each day is a fresh opportunity to experience the beauty of the world, nurture our relationships, and enhance our well-being. By taking a moment to express thanks to the Almighty, we set a positive tone for the day, embracing life with a heart full of appreciation. It is an invitation to consciously adopt this practice, recognizing that in doing so, we not only enhance our own lives but also contribute to a culture of gratitude and positivity in our families, communities, and the world at large.

87

Leading with Respect

Embracing and Celebrating Individuality

PSTO-87: Everyone is different, will have different needs, different aspirations, different ways of looking at things. Sooner a leader realises it, better it's for him as well as the whole team. 'Individuality' needs to be appreciated, honoured and celebrated too.

In the diverse tapestry of our world, every individual is unique, with distinct needs, aspirations, and perspectives. Effective leadership hinges on the ability to recognize, appreciate, honour, and celebrate this individuality. This chapter explores the importance of valuing and celebrating individuality within teams and organizations. Real-life examples illustrate how embracing diversity fosters innovation, inclusivity, and success.

1. Diversity Drives Innovation

Diversity of thought is not just a buzzword; it is a fundamental catalyst for innovation. In environments where individuals from various backgrounds, cultures, and perspectives come together, creativity flourishes. Silicon Valley serves as a prime example of this phenomenon, where tech giants like Google and Apple have built their success on diverse teams that bring unique viewpoints to the table. By encouraging collaboration among individuals with different experiences and ideas, these companies have been able to push the boundaries of technology, leading to groundbreaking advancements. This illustrates that when we embrace diversity, we unlock new potentials, enabling organizations to thrive and adapt in an ever-changing landscape..

2. Inclusivity Enhances Performance

Inclusivity is not merely a moral imperative; it significantly enhances performance within organizations. Indian Oil Corporation, the largest public sector enterprise in India, exemplifies this principle through its commitment to creating an inclusive workplace. By fostering an environment where employees from diverse backgrounds feel valued and respected, Indian Oil has experienced remarkable improvements in employee engagement and productivity. Initiatives that promote gender equality, support for differently-abled individuals, and the celebration of cultural diversity have contributed to a more dynamic workforce. Indian Oil has not only improved its operational efficiency but has also become a model for other organizations aiming to harness the power of inclusivity.

3. The Power of Individuality

The teachings of spiritual guru Ravi Shankar emphasize the profound power of individuality and the importance of respecting each person's unique contributions. He advocates for recognizing and celebrating the distinct qualities that every individual brings to the collective. According to Ravi Shankar, true leadership involves honoring these differences and creating a space where everyone can express themselves freely. His approach promotes the idea that when individuals feel accepted for who they are, they can tap into their full potential and contribute meaningfully to their communities.

Recognizing, appreciating, honouring, and celebrating individuality within teams and organizations is essential for success in today's diverse and interconnected world. The examples of Silicon Valley, Indian Oil Corporation and teachings of Ravi Shankar underscore the transformative power of embracing diversity and individuality. It is a reminder that diverse perspectives and experiences are valuable assets that drive innovation, inclusivity, and personal growth. By fostering an environment where every individual feels respected and celebrated, leaders not only empower their teams but also create a culture of excellence and collaboration. It is an invitation to lead with respect, acknowledging that it is our differences that make us stronger, more innovative, and better equipped to address the challenges and opportunities of our ever-evolving world. In celebrating individuality, we create a brighter future for all.

88

The Transformative Power of Accepting Mistakes

Building a Path to Growth

PSTO-88: We must learn to accept our mistakes. That lays the foundation of a corrective future. A mistake doesn't remain so when we accept and acknowledge it. It then becomes a great learning experience.

Mistakes are an inevitable part of the human experience, yet our willingness to accept and acknowledge them can be a transformative force. This chapter explores the importance of embracing our mistakes as valuable learning experiences that pave the way for growth and improvement. Some real-life examples illustrate how accepting mistakes can lead to personal and professional development.

1. The Value of Personal Growth

Accepting mistakes is a fundamental aspect of personal growth, exemplified by the journey of Pullela Gopichand, one of India's most celebrated badminton players and coaches. In his early career,

Gopichand faced significant setbacks, including injuries that threatened to derail his dreams of becoming a top player. Rather than succumbing to these challenges, he chose to view his mistakes and failures as valuable learning opportunities. Gopichand's willingness to confront his limitations and reflect on his experiences enabled him to refine his skills and develop a resilient mindset. This led him to achieve remarkable success, winning the prestigious All England Badminton Championship in 2001. Now, as a coach, he instills this lesson in his students, including world-class players like P.V. Sindhu and Saina Nehwal.

2. Leadership and Responsibility

Kumar Mangalam Birla faced criticism for the financial performance of his group's telecom venture, Idea Cellular, during the fierce competition in the Indian market. Instead of denying the mistakes made in strategic decisions, he accepted them and pivoted towards a merger with Vodafone India, which turned into a successful enterprise. Birla's willingness to acknowledge errors led to a stronger position in the telecom market, illustrating the power of learning from past decisions.

3. Personal Relationship

Accepting mistakes is vital for nurturing and strengthening personal relationships. The life of Lord Krishna, a revered figure in Hindu mythology, offers timeless lessons on this principle. One notable story involves Krishna accidentally breaking the precious Syamantaka jewel, which led to misunderstandings and distrust among his closest allies. Instead of denying his involvement or shifting blame, Krishna took responsibility for the incident and actively sought to rectify the situation. His humility and openness in accepting his mistake allowed him to restore harmony and trust within his circle. This narrative highlights that acknowledging our mistakes can lead to healing and deeper connections in our relationships.

Accepting and acknowledging mistakes is not a sign of weakness but a testament to our capacity for growth and improvement. The examples of Pulela Gopichand, Ratan Tata or Lord Krishna highlight the transformative power of embracing errors as learning experiences. It is a reminder that mistakes cease to be failures when we recognize and understand them. Instead, they become stepping stones to progress, innovation, and personal development. By fostering a culture that encourages individuals to take responsibility for their mistakes, leaders and individuals alike create an environment where growth and improvement flourish. It is an invitation to view mistakes not as setbacks but as opportunities for advancement, ultimately paving the way for a more successful and fulfilling future.

89

The Classroom of Life

Embracing Every Experience as a Lesson

PSTO-89: Every incident that happens in our lives or even around us teach us something new. It is on us to be conscious of it and take it as a positive learning.

Life is an ever-unfolding classroom, where every incident, whether in our own lives or around us, offers the opportunity to learn and grow. This chapter explores the importance of being conscious of the lessons embedded in our experiences and embracing them as valuable opportunities for positive learning. Real-life examples demonstrate how even challenging situations can be rich sources of wisdom and personal development.

1. The Wisdom in Adversity

Adversity often teaches the most profound lessons. Lal Bahadur Shastri, India's second Prime Minister, grew up facing severe financial struggles and personal hardships. Rather than being defeated by his circumstances, he used them as opportunities to develop resilience and humility. His early experiences with adversity shaped his leadership style, marked by simplicity and an unwavering commitment to the nation. When he led India during difficult times, including a war and food shortages, his calm demeanor and determination became sources of inspiration. Shastri's life demonstrates that the challenges we face often become the foundations of our greatest strengths, teaching us wisdom and endurance in the face of difficulties.

2. Personal Growth Through Self-Reflection

Ramakrishna Paramahansa, one of India's most influential spiritual figures, highlighted the power of self-reflection for personal growth. He believed that true wisdom comes from introspection and questioning one's beliefs. Ramakrishna's deep self-inquiry led him to the realization that different paths lead to the same ultimate truth, encouraging acceptance of all religious practices. Through continuous reflection, he cultivated self-awareness and inner peace, becoming a symbol of spiritual insight. His teachings emphasize that looking inward allows us to gain clarity, understand ourselves better, and foster compassion for others. Ramakrishna's example shows that self-reflection is a critical tool in the lifelong process of learning and evolving.

3. Learning from Mistakes

Mistakes are stepping stones to success, as illustrated by Ray Kroc, the man behind McDonald's global expansion. Before his triumph, Kroc encountered numerous failures in his business ventures. From unsuccessful ideas to misjudged strategies, each setback taught him valuable lessons. His ability to learn and adapt from his mistakes led him to refine the franchise model that eventually transformed McDonald's into a worldwide brand. Kroc's story highlights that success is rarely linear. Mistakes, while painful, provide critical learning experiences that help us improve and innovate. His journey underscores the importance of resilience and viewing failures as opportunities for growth rather than as final defeats.

Life's experiences, whether joyous or challenging, provide endless opportunities for learning and growth. The examples of Lal Bahadur Shastri, Ramakrishna Paramhansa and Ray Kroc illustrate the wisdom gained from adversity, the importance of self-reflection and the value of learning from mistakes. It is a reminder that every incident, large or small, carries a lesson if we are conscious and open to it. By embracing every experience as a positive learning opportunity, we enrich our lives and evolve into wiser, more compassionate, and resilient individuals. It is an invitation to view life as a continuous journey of growth and self-discovery, recognizing that the classroom of life is always open, and the lessons it imparts are boundless and transformative.

90

The Erosion of Innocence

Exploring the Journey from Childhood to Adulthood

PSTO-90: Are we not born innocent? Look at a baby and we see an ocean of innocence. Then how is it that we change as we grow up? Is it acquisition of knowledge or gaining of new experience or our greed for materialism that snatches away this innocence? We must ponder over it.

Babies are born into this world as pure and innocent beings, untouched by the complexities of life. However, as we grow and navigate the challenges of adulthood, our innocence can gradually erode. This essay delves into the factors that contribute to this transformation, including the acquisition of knowledge, life experiences, and the pursuit of materialism. Real-life examples shed light on how the loss of innocence is a natural part of the human journey, and yet, its essence can be preserved.

1. The Impact of Knowledge

While knowledge broadens our perspective, it often challenges our innocence. Albert Einstein's famous quote, "The more I learn, the more I realize how much I don't know," encapsulates the paradox of knowledge. As we gain understanding, we also become more aware of the complexities, injustices, and imperfections in the world around us. This awareness often dissolves the idealism of childhood, replacing it with a more nuanced, sometimes disheartening view of reality. Though essential for growth, the acquisition of knowledge pushes us to confront difficult truths, reshaping our perspectives and complicating the once-simple notions of good and bad that marked our early years.

2. The Pursuit of Materialism

The pursuit of material wealth can significantly erode the innocence we once cherished. In the movie Wall Street, Gordon Gekko's infamous line, "Greed, for lack of a better word, is good," symbolizes how the drive for success can overshadow personal values. The relentless chase for material gain, often seen as a marker of adulthood, pulls us away from the simplicity and purity of childhood. As we become entangled in the pressures of financial achievement, we risk losing sight of the non-material joys and ethical foundations that once defined us. This shift toward materialism reflects how easily innocence can be sacrificed in the name of ambition.

3. Reconnecting with Innocence

Despite the erosion of innocence, it is possible to reconnect with our pure inner self through spiritual and mindfulness practices. Teachings from spiritual leaders like the Dalai Lama advocate for compassion, forgiveness, and inner peace as pathways to preserving or rediscovering our essential innocence. Through meditation, self-reflection, and conscious living, we can detach from the distractions and pressures of modern life, allowing us to reconnect with the simpler, more authentic aspects of our being. These practices help us embrace a childlike wonder and purity, reminding us that, despite the challenges of adulthood, innocence can be reclaimed through intentional, mindful living.

The erosion of innocence is a natural part of the human journey, influenced by factors such as knowledge, life experiences, and the pursuit of materialism. The examples of Albert Einstein, Gordon Gekko, and the Dalai Lama shed light on this transformative process. While innocence may change as we grow, it need not be entirely lost. By embracing qualities like compassion, empathy, and inner peace, we can preserve our essential innocence even in the face of life's complexities. It is an invitation to reflect on the journey from childhood to adulthood, recognizing that while innocence may evolve, its essence can endure as a source of inspiration, kindness, and wonder in our lives.

91

Beyond Appearances

The Art of Recognizing Inner Qualities in Others

PSTO-91: How many times we must have heard, "Don't judge the book by the cover?" But we tend to be mostly driven by outward appearance and manifested behaviours of our friends and colleagues. For a leader, it is essential to understand the inner qualities or strengths of the team members. And sooner it is, the better.

The age-old wisdom advises us not to judge a book by its cover, yet our natural inclination often leads us to evaluate others based on outward appearances and visible behaviours. For leaders, the ability to discern the inner qualities and strengths of team members is essential. This chapter explores the importance of looking beyond the surface and understanding the profound potential that lies within individuals. Real-life examples demonstrate how recognizing inner qualities can lead to exceptional team dynamics and success.

1. The Deceptive Nature of Appearances

Appearances are often misleading, as demonstrated by the story of Susan Boyle, a Scottish singer who defied initial judgments on "Britain's Got Talent." When she first appeared on stage, her plain appearance led many to dismiss her talent. However, as soon as she began to sing, her extraordinary voice silenced critics and captivated millions. Boyle's journey is a powerful reminder that external appearances don't define a person's true abilities. Her success teaches us to look beyond the surface and recognize the hidden potential in others, showing that talent and character are often buried beneath superficial judgments.

2. Unearthing Hidden Talents

The story of Ekalavya from Indian mythology beautifully illustrates how inner strength and determination often surpass outward disadvantages. Born outside the elite class of warriors, Ekalavya was denied formal training by the renowned archer Dronacharya. However, through sheer determination and self-discipline, he taught himself archery by practicing in front of a statue of Dronacharya, becoming one of the greatest archers of his time. His story exemplifies that true talent and dedication can shine through despite societal barriers or lack of formal recognition. It reminds us to value determination and passion, which may often go unnoticed at first glance.

3. Encouraging Personal Growth

Sri Aurobindo's teachings emphasize the significance of looking beyond surface appearances to nurture inner development. He believed that true growth comes from tapping into one's inner potential and focusing on self-awareness and spiritual evolution. According to Sri Aurobindo, recognizing the soul's qualities, rather than just the external persona, is essential in fostering personal growth. This perspective encourages us to look within ourselves and others, fostering a deeper understanding of human potential. By acknowledging the innate qualities that lie beneath external traits, we can create an environment where personal transformation is prioritized over superficial achievements.

The adage "Don't judge the book by the cover" serves as a reminder that appearances can be misleading. The examples of Susan Boyle, Ekalavya, and Sri Aurobindo underscore the transformative power of recognizing inner qualities in others. For leaders, understanding the strengths and potential of team members is not only essential but also the key to unlocking exceptional team dynamics and success. It is an invitation to practice empathy, nurture hidden talents, and inspire personal growth by looking beyond the surface and embracing the rich tapestry of human potential. By doing so, leaders create environments where every individual's unique qualities are acknowledged, valued, and leveraged to achieve collective greatness.

92

Embracing Change

The Virtue That Ensures Survival in a New World

PSTO-92: 'Adapting to the change' is a virtue, which we all probably would have to get imbibed in ourselves as well as in our near and dear ones. This virtue can only let us survive the new order.

In a world characterized by constant evolution and transformation, the ability to adapt to change has become a vital virtue. This chapter explores the importance of embracing change not only in our own lives but also in those of our loved ones. Real-life examples illustrate how this virtue is the key to not just survival but thriving in the ever-evolving landscape of our world.

1. The Resilience of Nature

Nature teaches us that resilience and adaptability are key to survival. The Galápagos Islands are home to unique species that have evolved over centuries to thrive in diverse and challenging environments. Charles Darwin's observations of these islands laid the foundation for the theory of evolution, emphasizing how species must adapt to changing conditions to survive. For example, the beak shapes of finches evolved based on the availability of food sources. Nature's inherent ability to adjust to environmental shifts offers us a profound lesson: flexibility and openness to change are essential for survival, especially in an ever-evolving world.

2. Thriving in Technology

In today's fast-paced world, embracing technological change is crucial for success. Jeff Bezos, founder of Amazon, exemplifies this through his foresight in transforming the retail industry. From its beginnings as an online bookstore, Amazon evolved into a global marketplace, adapting to the changing needs of consumers. Bezos recognized that innovation was key to survival, continually investing in technology to improve logistics, customer service, and cloud computing. His ability to adapt not only disrupted traditional retail but also set a new standard for e-commerce. Bezos' journey highlights how embracing change in technology can drive unprecedented success and growth.

3. Adapting as a Community

Communities that adapt to changing circumstances are the ones that thrive. Bhutan offers a remarkable example of this through its philosophy of "Gross National Happiness" (GNH). In a world driven by GDP and material wealth, Bhutan shifted its focus to well-being and sustainability. GNH emphasizes spiritual, emotional, and environmental health, ensuring that development is balanced with happiness. This innovative approach has allowed Bhutan to adapt its values to prioritize the well-being of its people and environment. By focusing on holistic happiness, the country has created a sustainable model for community adaptation in the face of global challenges.

Embracing change is not merely a virtue; it is a necessity in our ever-evolving world. The examples of the Galápagos Islands, Jeff Bezos, and Bhutan underscore the transformative power of adaptation. It is a reminder that change is an inherent part of life and that by embracing it, we not only survive but thrive. To adapt is to remain open to new possibilities, to learn from experiences, and to grow as individuals and communities. It is an invitation to cultivate this virtue in ourselves and encourage it in our loved ones, recognizing that in doing so, we prepare ourselves not just to endure change but to flourish in a new world filled with opportunities and possibilities.

93

Embracing Life's Spectrum

Finding Meaning in Its Diverse Hues

PSTO-93: Life comes with different hues and each one of these has different meaning, different connotations, different importance for each one of us. It is, therefore, incumbent on us to take advantage of each of the hues and enjoy.

Life is a canvas painted with a myriad of hues, each carrying its own unique meaning, connotation, and significance to every individual. This chapter explores the importance of recognizing and appreciating the diverse experiences that life offers. Real-life examples illustrate how embracing the richness of these hues leads to a more fulfilling and meaningful existence.

1. The Diversity of Emotions

Life is enriched by the wide spectrum of emotions we experience, much like the complex characters in William Shakespeare's works. From the depths of despair in Hamlet to the joy of love in Romeo and Juliet, Shakespeare masterfully portrayed the full range of human emotions, showing us that each feeling has its place and value. His characters teach us that embracing every emotion, whether happiness, sorrow, or anger, allows us to fully experience life's richness. Just as a play becomes more compelling with a diversity of emotions, so too does life become more meaningful when we allow ourselves to feel and grow through each experience.

2. The Spectrum of Relationships

Relationships, with their many layers and complexities, contribute significantly to the richness of life. Jean-Paul Sartre and Simone de Beauvoir, both influential philosophers and writers, shared a deep romantic and intellectual bond while maintaining their independence. Their relationship exemplified how love can coexist with personal growth and creative freedom. They supported and challenged each other, making their bond a source of mutual enrichment rather than limitation. Like their partnership, relationships in life often bring contrasting emotions, yet they shape who we are and provide us with the opportunity to grow through connection, understanding, and acceptance.

3. The Shades of Personal Growth

Personal growth is not a linear journey but a process filled with ups and downs, as demonstrated by Indian hockey player Sandeep Singh. After being paralyzed by an accidental gunshot, Singh faced a life-altering challenge but refused to let it define him. Through intense determination and resilience, he not only recovered but made a successful comeback to the national team, becoming an inspiration for many. His story illustrates that life's struggles are part of the spectrum of growth, and that setbacks can serve as the catalysts for greater achievements. Each shade of adversity can paint a new layer of strength and growth in our lives.

Life is a masterpiece, and each of us is an artist with our own palette of experiences. The examples of William Shakespeare, Jean-Paul Sartre, Simone de Beauvoir, and Sandeep Singh illustrate the richness that embracing life's diverse hues can bring. It is a reminder that every emotion, relationship, challenge, and cultural encounter adds depth and meaning to our existence. By savouring each colour on the canvas of life, we create a more fulfilling and meaningful journey. It is an invitation to celebrate the diversity of experiences, recognizing that in doing so, we unlock the full spectrum of life's beauty, wisdom, and joy.

94

Managing Expectations

The Key to Finding True Self-Worth

PSTO-94: We can and must manage our expectations. But it may not be feasible to live up to others'. As long as we are happy and convinced about the 'person in the mirror', we need not probably worry what others expect from us or think about us.

In a world where external expectations often weigh heavily on our shoulders, the ability to manage our own expectations and prioritize our own happiness is essential. This chapter delves into the importance of finding contentment in being true to oneself rather than trying to meet the expectations others may have. Real-life examples highlight how embracing one's authentic self leads to genuine happiness and self-worth.

1. The Weight of External Expectations

External expectations can weigh heavily on individuals, shaping their lives in ways that often lead to inner conflict. Princess Diana is a poignant example. Thrust into the public eye with the pressures of royalty, she struggled to balance her personal identity with the demands of the British monarchy. Despite her public role and the image she was expected to maintain, Diana sought personal happiness beyond the confines of royal expectations. Her journey highlights how the pressure to conform to others' ideals can erode one's sense of self-worth, reminding us of the importance of aligning our actions with our true selves rather than the expectations of others.

2. The Power of Authenticity

Sardar Vallabhbhai Patel, the Iron Man of India, exemplified the power of authenticity in the face of expectations. Despite pressures to follow more radical approaches during India's independence movement, Patel stayed true to his pragmatic and steadfast nature, focusing on unifying India through diplomacy and firmness. His authenticity earned him respect and trust, making him a pivotal figure in the country's history. Patel's unwavering belief in his principles teaches us that staying true to oneself, even when others expect otherwise, leads to genuine respect and long-lasting impact. His life stands as a testament to the power of authenticity in defining self-worth.

3. The Pursuit of Happiness

In *The Monk Who Sold His Ferrari*, Robin Sharma delves into the concept of true happiness, emphasizing that it is not found in material wealth or meeting societal expectations, but in inner peace and self-fulfillment. The protagonist, a high-powered lawyer, gives up his affluent lifestyle to discover deeper meaning in life. Through his journey, we learn that happiness stems from living authentically, focusing on personal growth, and embracing a simpler, more purposeful existence. Sharma's story reminds us that happiness is not a product of success or external validation but comes from aligning with our core values and finding contentment within.

Managing our own expectations and finding happiness in the reflection in the mirror are essential components of self-worth.

The examples of Princess Diana, Sardar Patel, and the learnings from Robin Sharma's book demonstrate the transformative power of embracing authenticity and prioritizing personal happiness. It is a reminder that living up to others' expectations may lead to external validation, but true self-worth comes from being authentic and content with the person we see in the mirror. By cultivating self-acceptance and embracing our unique path in life, we discover a deeper, more meaningful sense of worth that can withstand the pressures of external judgments. It is an invitation to prioritize inner happiness and self-validation over the fleeting expectations of others, recognizing that our worth is ultimately defined by our own standards, values, and authenticity.

95

The Power of Positivity

Illuminating the Path to Positive Outcomes

PSTO-95: We must always try to stay positive, irrespective of the current situation we are going through. I also realise and accept it is difficult. But it's positive too. We must have faith that Positivity brings Positive outcomes at the end.

In the face of life's challenges, maintaining a positive outlook can be a beacon of hope and resilience. This chapter explores the significance of staying positive even in difficult circumstances, with a belief that positivity can ultimately yield positive outcomes. Real-life examples showcase how unwavering optimism can lead to transformative results.

1. The Triumph of Positive Thinking

Shrikant Bolla, a blind entrepreneur who faced numerous challenges, exemplifies the power of positive thinking. Born into a poor family, Shrikant encountered prejudice and rejection throughout his life, including being denied entry to prestigious Indian institutions because of his disability. Yet, he never let negativity overshadow his vision. Shrikant pursued education abroad, excelling at MIT, and eventually founded Bollant Industries, a company that employs hundreds of people with disabilities. His story demonstrates how a positive mindset can transform adversity into opportunity. By focusing on his abilities rather than his limitations, Shrikant has become a beacon of hope, proving that optimism can pave the way to success.

2. Overcoming Personal Obstacles

Murlikant Petkar, India's first Paralympic gold medalist, is a powerful example of resilience and positivity in the face of personal challenges. A soldier injured during the 1965 Indo-Pak war, Petkar was left disabled, but he refused to be defined by his physical limitations. His perseverance and unwavering spirit led him to swimming, where he broke records and won India's first gold medal at the 1972 Paralympics. Petkar's journey illustrates how overcoming personal obstacles with determination and positivity can lead to extraordinary achievements, turning setbacks into stepping stones for success. His triumph reminds us that a positive attitude can fuel the drive to achieve greatness.

3. Inspiring Collective Change

Raja Ram Mohan Roy, a pioneer of social reform in India, is a shining example of how positivity and progressive thinking can inspire collective change. During the early 19th century, Roy fought against social injustices like sati (the burning of widows), child marriage, and rigid caste distinctions. Despite opposition from traditionalists, his unwavering belief in progress and human dignity helped transform Indian society. Through education and advocacy, he laid the foundation for modern Indian reforms, championing women's rights and promoting rationalism. Roy's life shows that a positive vision, coupled with courage and persistence, can mobilize communities and drive societal change for the better.

Staying positive in the face of adversity is a beacon of hope and resilience. The examples of Shrikant Bolla, Murlikant Petkar and Raja Ram Mohan Roy illustrate the transformative power of unwavering optimism. It is a reminder that positivity is not just a state of mind but a catalyst for positive outcomes. By embracing a positive outlook and having faith that it can lead to transformative results, we not only uplift ourselves but also inspire others and create a ripple effect of optimism in the world. It is an invitation to choose positivity, recognizing that it has the potential to illuminate the darkest of paths and ultimately lead to positive, impactful outcomes.

96

The Power of Awareness

Shaping a Conscious and Informed Society

PSTO-96: It is extremely essential for each one of us to be aware of what is happening around us, irrespective of the fact whether it affects us directly or not.

In an interconnected world, awareness of our surroundings is not merely a choice but a responsibility. This chapter delves into the significance of being cognizant of what is happening around us, even when it may not have a direct impact. Real-life examples highlight how awareness can lead to informed decisions, positive change, and a more engaged and compassionate society.

1. The Ripple Effect of Awareness

Awareness has the power to ignite widespread change, as seen in the work of environmentalist Rachel Carson. Her groundbreaking book, Silent Spring, exposed the harmful effects of pesticides on ecosystems, particularly highlighting the dangers of DDT. By raising awareness of these issues, Carson sparked the modern environmental movement, which led to significant policy changes, including the eventual ban on DDT in many countries. Her efforts remind us that awareness can act as a catalyst for social and environmental reform. Through her message, Carson inspired generations to take responsibility for preserving the planet, proving that informed awareness can transform society on a large scale.

2. Social Change Through Awareness

Kamala Pujari, a tribal woman from Odisha, exemplifies how awareness can bring about significant social change. Despite her humble beginnings, Pujari's work in promoting indigenous farming techniques and preserving traditional rice varieties raised awareness about sustainable agriculture. Her contributions earned her national recognition, proving that awareness at the grassroots level can lead to meaningful change. By advocating for the use of organic farming methods and indigenous seeds, she not only empowered her community but also influenced agricultural practices across India. Pujari's journey shows that awareness of local knowledge and environmental sustainability can shape healthier, more resilient societies.

3. Global Citizenship and Responsibility

Awareness plays a vital role in fostering global citizenship, as evidenced during the COVID-19 pandemic. The crisis highlighted how interconnected we are, with the virus spreading rapidly across borders and affecting every aspect of life worldwide. Global awareness of the pandemic's impact led to unprecedented collaboration among nations, scientific communities, and healthcare professionals to develop solutions. It also reinforced the importance of personal responsibility—wearing masks, practicing social distancing, and getting vaccinated to protect not only ourselves but others as well. The pandemic emphasized that a well-informed and conscious global society is essential for navigating shared challenges and ensuring collective well-being.

Awareness is not just an individual choice; it is a responsibility that shapes our society and our world. The examples of Rachel

Carson, Kamala Pujari and the global response to the COVID-19 pandemic illustrate the transformative power of awareness. It is a reminder that being informed about what is happening around us, even when it may not directly impact us, empowers us to make informed decisions, contribute to positive change, and create a more engaged and compassionate society. It is an invitation to embrace our role as informed and responsible citizens of the world, recognizing that awareness is the first step toward meaningful action and progress.

97

The Wisdom of Retreat

Finding Clarity in Taking a Step Backward

PSTO-97: Taking a step backward when there is lack of clarity is perhaps the best step forward. It's not regressive, rather it's the best possible positive alternative.

In a world that often celebrates relentless forward motion, the wisdom of taking a step backward to gain clarity is often underestimated. This chapter explores the value of retreat as a means of finding clarity and making informed decisions. Real-life examples highlight how stepping back is not regressive but can be the most positive and proactive choice in the face of uncertainty.

1. The Art of Strategic Retreat

Strategic retreat has long been recognized as a vital element of effective military leadership. General George Washington exemplified this during the American Revolutionary War when he made the tough decision to retreat from New York City in 1776. Instead of risking his troops in a losing battle, Washington regrouped and re-strategized, preserving the Continental Army for future engagements. This decision ultimately allowed him to orchestrate significant victories, including the surprise attack on Trenton. Washington's ability to recognize when to step back not only saved his army but also turned the tide of the war, demonstrating that retreating strategically can lead to greater long-term success.

2. Seeking Clarity Through Meditation

Meditation is a powerful tool for finding clarity and inner peace, as taught by the renowned spiritual leader Osho. He emphasized the importance of retreating from the chaos of daily life to connect with one's inner self. Through meditation, individuals can step back from their thoughts, allowing them to gain perspective on their emotions and challenges. Osho advocated for regular meditation practices as a means of self-discovery and personal transformation, encouraging followers to explore their inner landscapes. This form of retreat fosters clarity, enabling individuals to make informed decisions and approach life's complexities with a calm, centered mindset, ultimately leading to a more fulfilling existence.

3. The "Pause Button" in Decision-making

In *Reset: A Leader's Guide to Work in an Age of Upheaval*, Johnny C. Taylor Jr. explores the necessity of taking a pause in decision-making, especially during turbulent times. He argues that a strategic retreat allows leaders to reassess situations, gather insights, and avoid impulsive decisions driven by stress or uncertainty. By pressing the "pause button," leaders can reflect on their values, goals, and the impact of their choices on their teams. Taylor's insights underscore that embracing moments of retreat can lead to better decision-making, ultimately enhancing organizational resilience. In a fast-paced world, taking a step back is essential for thoughtful and effective leadership.

Taking a step backward in pursuit of clarity is not a sign of regression but a proactive choice for growth and informed decision-making. The examples of General George Washington, Meditation by Osho and the learning from book of Johnny Taylor illustrate how strategic retreat, whether in leadership, personal development, or decision-making, can lead to transformative outcomes. It is a reminder that in moments of uncertainty, stepping back can provide a fresh perspective, preserve vital resources, and lead to more calculated and successful forward movements. It is an invitation to embrace the wisdom of retreat as a positive alternative, recognizing that clarity often emerges from moments of pause and reflection.

98

The Power of Commitment
Fuelling Passion and Achievement

PSTO-98: Commitment is a virtue, which we must try to imbibe. Our commitment to targets or gaols define our mental framework, our preparedness and our passion.

Commitment is the driving force that propels us toward our goals and aspirations. This chapter explores the significance of commitment as a virtue, emphasizing how our unwavering dedication to targets or goals shapes our mindset, preparedness, and passion. Real-life examples illuminate the transformative power of commitment in achieving remarkable success.

1. Entrepreneurial Commitment and Innovation

Anand Mahindra, the Chairman of the Mahindra Group, exemplifies the power of commitment in driving innovation and entrepreneurship. His steadfast dedication to fostering a culture of sustainability and social responsibility has transformed his company into a global powerhouse. Under his leadership, Mahindra has embraced innovative technologies, such as electric vehicles and digital solutions, positioning itself at the forefront of industry evolution. Mahindra's commitment to not just profit but also to community welfare and environmental stewardship has led to groundbreaking initiatives like the Mahindra Rise campaign, demonstrating that a passionate commitment to values can inspire innovation while making a positive impact on society.

2. Commitment in Sports and Excellence

Rishabh Pant, the young Indian cricketer, exemplifies the commitment required for excellence in sports. His journey from a budding talent to a key player in the Indian national team showcases his unwavering dedication and hard work. In late 2022, Pant faced a life-threatening accident, which could have derailed his career. Instead, he showed remarkable resilience in his recovery, committing himself to rigorous rehabilitation and training. His determination to return to the field highlights the profound impact of personal commitment. Pant's remarkable performances, including record-breaking innings, serve as a powerful reminder that overcoming adversity through passion and perseverance can inspire teammates and fans alike, fostering a culture of excellence.

3. The Role of Personal Commitment

Baba Kalyani faced significant challenges while expanding Bharat Forge from a small Indian forging company to a global player in the automotive and aerospace sectors. His personal commitment to innovation and quality was unwavering, even when the company encountered financial setbacks. Kalyani invested heavily in research and development, ensuring that Bharat Forge kept pace with technological advancements. His commitment not only helped the company survive tough times but also transformed it into a leading supplier of components for major international clients, showcasing how dedication to goals can drive success.

Commitment is the bedrock of achievement, passion, and personal growth. The examples of Anand Mahindra, Rishabh Pant and Usain Bolt underscore the transformative power of unwavering dedication to targets or goals. It is a reminder that commitment defines our mental framework, fuels our preparedness, and ignites our passion. By embracing commitment as a virtue, we not only set ourselves on a path to success but also inspire others and drive positive change in the world. It is an invitation to cultivate commitment in our pursuits, recognizing that it is the force that propels us toward greatness and shapes the future we aspire to create.

99

Reflecting on Words and Actions

A Path to Personal Growth and Positive Impact

PSTO-99: Do we ever replay our words or actions in our mind? We must purposely do that, understand the effects of our words or actions on our ecosystem. That will provide us invaluable cues on how not to repeat some of our words or actions.

Our words and actions have a profound impact not only on ourselves but also on the ecosystem we are part of. This chapter explores the importance of purposefully reflecting on our words and actions, understanding their effects, and using this awareness as a catalyst for personal growth and positive change. Real-life examples illustrate how conscious reflection can lead to more mindful behaviour.

1. The Ripple Effect of Words

Words have the power to shape thoughts, beliefs, and actions, echoing across generations. Ancient Hindu scriptures, such as the Bhagavad Gita and Upanishads, emphasize the significance of speech and its potential to uplift or harm. The Gita teaches that words can inspire righteous action and foster understanding, while careless speech can lead to discord and confusion. This profound understanding illustrates the ripple effect of words; when individuals choose their words mindfully, they can create waves of positivity that impact those around them. By reflecting on the intention and consequences behind our words, we can cultivate an environment of respect, kindness, and encouragement, enhancing personal growth and fostering harmonious relationships.

2. Actions as a Catalyst for Change

Actions often serve as powerful catalysts for societal transformation. Harshita Mohanty, known as the "Seed Girl," exemplifies this principle through her dedication to environmental sustainability. After witnessing the adverse effects of deforestation in her community, Harshita began her 'seed' journey a few years back. She collected all the paddy and millet seeds from different haats and farmers of Jeypore, Boipariguda, Kundra and Borrigumma blocks of the district, and continues to do so to date. Subsequently, she set up a foodgrain and seed bank at her house where the seeds and food grains are safely stored in glass bottles. Her story emphasizes how committed actions can lead to significant change, encouraging others to reflect on their role in creating a better world. Such initiatives highlight that individual efforts can collectively make a substantial impact on society.

3. Creating a Culture of Reflection

Creating a culture of reflection is essential for fostering personal and communal growth. Sadguru Jaggi Vasudev teaches that introspection allows individuals to understand their thoughts and behaviors, leading to profound self-awareness. By incorporating regular reflection into our daily routines, we can critically assess our words and actions, recognizing patterns that may require change. This practice cultivates mindfulness and empathy, enabling individuals to respond thoughtfully rather than react impulsively. Furthermore, promoting reflection within communities encourages open dialogue and shared learning, leading to stronger relationships and collaborative problem-solving. As people embrace this culture, they contribute to a more conscious and compassionate society, where personal growth is intertwined with positive societal impact.

Conscious reflection on our words and actions is a catalyst for personal growth, positive impact, and more mindful behavior. The learnings from ancient scriptures, Harshita Mohanty, the seed girl and teachings of Sadguru show the transformative power of intentional reflection. It is a reminder that understanding the effects of our words and actions on our ecosystem allows us to become more mindful and empathetic individuals. By purposefully replaying our interactions and using the cues for self-improvement, we not only become better versions of ourselves but also contribute to a more harmonious and compassionate world. It is an invitation to embrace reflection as a tool for personal growth and positive change, recognizing that every word and action has the potential to shape our lives and the lives of those around us.

100

Defining Character Through Values

Living a Life of Purpose

PSTO-100: We may not be what others see us as. We may not be what we do for our living. We are defined by the values we create, values we stand for and values, we live. Our value system defines us.

In a world often preoccupied with external appearances and professions, the essence of an individual lies in their values. This chapter explores the profound impact of values on one's character and identity, emphasizing that we are defined not by what we do for a living or how others perceive us but by the values we create, stand for, and live by. Real-life examples illustrate how values shape a person's identity and legacy.

1. The Power of Integrity

Integrity is a cornerstone of character, shaping how individuals are perceived and how they impact the world. Netaji Subhas Chandra Bose exemplified integrity in his unwavering commitment to India's independence. Despite facing immense challenges, including opposition from colonial powers and within his own ranks, Bose remained steadfast in his beliefs. He prioritized the nation's freedom over personal gain, making significant sacrifices for the cause. His authenticity and dedication inspired countless others to join the struggle for independence. Bose's life teaches us that integrity is not merely about adhering to moral principles but also about being true to one's convictions, even in the face of adversity.

2. Values as a Guiding Light

Values serve as a guiding light, steering individuals toward meaningful lives. Utkalamani Gopabandhu Das, a revered figure from Odisha, embodied the values of service, education, and social justice. He dedicated his life to uplifting the marginalized and promoting education for all, particularly in rural areas. He believed that true progress comes from empowering communities through knowledge and self-reliance. His actions reflected a deep commitment to the welfare of others, inspiring generations to prioritize collective growth over personal ambition. By living according to his values, Das not only shaped his character but also left an indelible mark on society, reminding us that values are the foundation upon which purpose is built.

3. A Lasting Impact Through Generosity

Generosity is a powerful expression of character, shaping one's legacy and influence on future generations. Andrew Carnegie, a prominent philanthropist, exemplified this through his commitment to using his wealth for the greater good. After achieving immense success in the steel industry, he dedicated his later years to funding educational initiatives, libraries, and cultural institutions. Carnegie believed that access to knowledge was crucial for individual and societal advancement. His philanthropic endeavors established countless libraries and learning opportunities, significantly impacting communities across the globe. Carnegie's legacy illustrates how generosity can create lasting change, demonstrating that true fulfillment comes from giving back and uplifting others.

Our values, the principles we create, stand for, and live by, define our true character and identity. The examples of Netaji Subhash Chandra Bose, Utkalamani Gopabandhu Das and Andrew Carnegie depict the profound impact of values on an individual's legacy. It is a reminder that, regardless of our profession or external appearances, it is our values that leave a lasting mark on the world. By cultivating and embodying values that reflect our true essence, we not only define ourselves but also inspire positive change and leave a legacy that transcends time. It is an invitation to live a life of purpose, guided by the values that resonate with our hearts, recognizing that it is through our values that we make a lasting impact on the world and the lives we touch.

Epilogue

Life is full of learning. The more we keep our mind open, we would tend to observe so many things all around us, which would not only help us to learn quite a few things, it may also give a completely new perspective to life. As a self-proclaimed Learner for Life, my efforts to continue to keep my quest alive shall continue.

I would like to end this with one of my linkedin Post about someone I met during a trip to Amritsar.

Quote

Today, I had this enchanting encounter in Amritsar.

We went out for a dinner. After looking for some online recommendations as well as recommended by some friends, we zeroed on Surjeet Food Plaza. Must thank Rakesh, who himself is a vegetarian and Pratham, who was on fast, to have organised this.

Thankfully, I had Prof Dr. Jeeta to give me company in this non-vegetarian sojourn. That's a different matter. It's not about my foody adventure. It's all about Amarjeet Singh, the proprietor cum chef cum usherer, all rolled into one, in that small yet fabulous eating joint named "Surjit Food Plaza". The fact that the food we ate was simply superb, is not again the matter.

The point in contention was how Amarjeet simply sold it to us.

This is what I always say, we don't teach in our B-Schools.

He was enterprising, he was plain, simple, ever smiling yet very firm; firm in his conviction about his items, about his restaurant and overall about his own demeanor as well. It was a 'killing confidence' and this is what no B-School teaches.

He endeared himself in seconds, not only to us, but also to all other customers, who had come to his restaurant.

He made us eat more than what we would have normally eaten (in fact, Dr. Jeeta admitted that she ate mutton after umpteen years), he made us eat whatever he proposed and he did all these with us never feeling the same, rather making us convinced that it was purely our decision.

And finally like a true management expert, he takes our feedback in his own inimitable way, where feedback felt like endorsement, very naturally.

It was a big Case Study for me and the team. We all agreed, unanimously, that we all saw the best management lesson in practice.

It was such a pleasure meeting Amarjeet, the enterprising Manager, who never went to a Management School. Thank you Amarjeet for showing us what we are probably lacking in our Management Education.

#Management #Learning #Leadership #Education #ConsciousLeadership

UnQuote

List of Examples (In Alphabetical Order)

Sr. No.	Name	Chapter #
57	Desmond Tutu	33
58	Didier Drogba	23
59	Doctors without Borders	23
60	Dolly Parton	15
61	Dr APJ Abdul Kalam	25, 48
62	Dr Andrew Weil	42
63	Dr Brené Brown	25,46
64	Dr Ignaz Semmelweis	79
65	Dr Jane Goodall	12
66	Dr Kristin Neff	25
67	Dr Laura Markham	25
68	Dr Manoj Kumar Sharma	84
69	Dr Paul Farmer	24, 63
70	Dr Robert Emmons	66
71	Dr V Shanta	64
72	Dr Vikram Sarabhai	82
73	Dwight D Eisenhower	41
74	Eat Pray Love	35
75	Edmund Hillary	58
76	Eduardo Saverin	74
77	Eklavya	91
78	Eleanor Roosevelt	62
79	Eliud Kipchoge	38
80	Elizabeth Holmes	16
81	Ellen DeGeneres	64
82	Elon Musk	12, 22
83	Emma Watson	62
84	Fali Nariman	57
85	Francesco Cirillo	41
86	Francis Crick	29
87	Fred Rodgers	15
88	Garry Kasparov	72
89	Gayle King	37
90	George Clooney	79
91	George Washington	97
92	Georgia O'Keeffe	24
93	Gitanjali Rao	53
94	Google	15, 30, 68, 72
95	Gopabandhu Das	100
96	Gopal Krishna Gokhale	54
97	Gorden Gekko	90
98	Greg Mortenson	36
99	Greta Thunberg	28
100	Gross National Happiness (GNH)	92
101	Hanuman	2
102	Harish Hande	28
103	Harshita Mohanty	99
104	Harvey Milk	62
105	Helen Keller	67
106	Henry David Thoreau	39
107	Henry Ford	76
108	Hermann Kallenbach	37
109	Howard Hughes	60
110	Howard Schultz	67
111	Implicit Association Test (IAT)	30
112	Indian Oil Corporation	87

Sr. No.	Name	Chapter #
113	Indra Nooyi	43
114	Irom Sharmila	53
115	Isaac Newton	3
116	ISRO	70
117	JK Rowling	1, 52
118	JRR Tolkien	67
119	Jacinda Ardern	18, 73
120	Jadav Payeng	78
121	Jaime Escalante	8
122	James Watson	29
123	Jamshedji Tata	49
124	Jean-Paul Sartre	93
125	Jeff Bezos	92
126	Jeff Immelt	67
127	Jeff Weiner	52
128	Jim Carrey	55
129	Jimmy Carter	33
130	Jiro Ono	52
131	John Krasinski	64
132	John Wooden	63
133	Johnny C Taylor Jr	97
134	Johny Wilkinson	71
135	Jon Kabat-Zinn	69
136	Joseph Stalin	37
137	Julia Child	64
138	Julius Caesar	4
139	Jürgen Klopp	68
140	Justin Bieber	16
141	Kailash Satyarthi	40
142	Kalpana Chawla	54
143	Kamala Pujari	96

Sr. No.	Name	Chapter #
144	Keanu Reeves	64
145	Kiran Bedi	59
146	Kobe Bryant	32
147	Kofi Annan	57
148	Kumar Mangalam Birla	88
149	Lal Bahadur Shastri	73, 89
150	Lata Mangeshkar	48
151	Laxman Rao	40
152	LeBron James	14
153	Leonardo da Vinci	6
154	Lewis Hamilton	54
155	Linus Torvalds	29
156	Lionel Messi	55
157	Lord Ganesha	2
158	Lord Krishna	2, 88
159	Louis Zamperini	34
160	MS Dhoni	14, 27
161	MS Swaminathan	40
162	Madhusudan Das	85
163	Mahadevi Verma	57
164	Mahatma Gandhi	15, 37, 57, 77
165	Malala Yousafzai	11, 52
166	Marcus Rashford	36
167	Mark Andreessen	29
168	Mark Zuckerberg	21, 74
169	Mars Rover	29
170	Martin Luther King Jr	11, 77
171	Mary Kom	26
172	Mary McLeod Bethune	78

Sr. No.	Name	Chapter #
173	Maya Angelou	17
174	Menachem Begin	33
175	Michael Jackson	46
176	Michael Jordan	31, 52, 60
177	Michael Phelps	24,59
178	Michelangelo	80
179	Michelle Obama	34
180	MAAS	39
181	MBSR	42
182	Mithali Raj	46
183	Mohammad Azharuddin	74
184	Morrie Schwartz	86
185	Mother Teresa	22, 49
186	Murlikant Petkar	95
187	Naomi Osaka	69
188	Narayana Murthy	40
189	Narendra Modi	84
190	NASA	9
191	NASA Challenger	75, 79
192	Neeraj Chopra	31
193	Nelson Mandela	1, 17, 57
194	Nicholas Winton	28
195	Nick Vujicic	34
196	Oklahoma City Firefighter	83
197	Oprah Winfrey	26, 37
198	Osho	97
199	Oskar Schindler	36
200	PV Sindhu	80
201	Pablo Picasso	12

Sr. No.	Name	Chapter #
202	Pat Cummins	80
203	Paulo Coelho	11
204	Peace Corp	19
205	Phil Jackson	9
206	Pixar Animation Studios	14
207	Play Pump Water System	79
208	Prince Harry	74
209	Prince William	74
210	Princess Diana	94
211	Pulela Gopichand	88
212	Queen	35
213	Rachel Carson	96
214	Raja Harishchandra	73
215	Raja Ram Mohan Roy	53, 95
216	Ramakrishna Paramhansa	89
217	Ratan Tata	40, 60
218	Ravi Shankar	87
219	Ray Kroc	89
220	Richard Branson	20, 22
221	Rishabh Pant	98
222	Robin Sharma	94
223	Rocket Man	35
224	Roger Federer	59, 71
225	Rohit Sharma	24
226	Rosa Parks	62
227	Rosalind Franklin	29
228	Rosie the Riveter	81
229	Ruskin Bond	19
230	Ruth Bader Ginsburg	73

Sr. No.	Name	Chapter #
231	Sachin Tendulkar	17
232	Sadguru Jaggi Vasudev	99
233	Salman "Sal" Khan	32
234	Sandeep Singh	93
235	Sanjay Dutt	46
236	Sara Blakely	38
237	Sardar Patel	94
238	Satyajit Ray	48
239	Serena Williams	16, 58
240	Sheryl Sandberg	21, 30
241	Shinrin-yoku (Forest Bathing)	39
242	Shiv Khera	58
243	Shrikant Bolla	95
244	Silicon Valley	3, 9, 87
245	Simone Biles	42
246	Simone de Beauvoir	93
247	Sir Alex Ferguson	18
248	Sir David Attenborough	31
249	Sir Ken Robinson	72
250	Sir Tim Berners-Lee	29
251	Slumdog Millionaire	35
252	Sonam Wangchuk	23
253	SpaceX	5
254	Sri Aurobindo	91
255	Srinivasa Ramanujan	23
256	Stephen Hawking	32
257	Stephen King	41
258	Steve Jobs	14, 37
259	Steven Gerrard	71

Sr. No.	Name	Chapter #
260	Subhash Ch Bose	100
261	Subway Therapy	27
262	Sudha Murty	19
263	Suhas Yathiraj	84
264	Sumit Agarwal	34
265	Sundar Pichai	58
266	Sunil Gavaskar	70
267	Susan Boyle	91
268	Swami Vivekananda	75
269	Tara Westover	21
270	Taylor Swift	66
271	Teladoc	76
272	Temie Giwa-Tubosun	38
273	Temple Grandin	32, 47
274	Tenzing Norgay	58
275	Tesla	29, 76
276	The Beatles	68
277	Thich Nhat Hanh	42
278	Thimmakka	78
279	Thomas Edison	1
280	Tim Cook	43
281	Titanic	74
282	Tom Brady	38
283	Tom Hanks	43, 78
284	Tony Hsieh	8
285	Tony Robbins	46
286	US Space Program	18
287	Usain Bolt	19, 61
288	Valmik Thapar	39
289	Vijay Amritraj	27
290	Viktor Frankl	60, 65

Sr. No.	Name	Chapter #
291	Vincent van Gogh	4, 82
292	Vinoba Bhave	82
293	Virat Kohli	61
294	Viswanathan Anand	63
295	Voyager 1 & 2	6
296	Wadata Talak Safety Net Programme	83
297	Walt Disney	55
298	Warren Buffett	17, 20
299	Will Smith	59
300	William Shakespeare	6, 93
301	Winston Churchill	13, 37
302	Wright Brothers	1, 68
303	Y Combinator	68
304	Yuvraj Singh	65
305	Zappos	14, 81

Dr. Ranjan Kumar Mohapatra, a visionary leader and empathetic thinker, brings a unique blend of strategic insight and human-centric leadership. As the former Director (Human Resources) of Indian Oil, he led over thirty-one thousand employees, driving initiatives that transformed the organization into a learning powerhouse with Swadhyaya, India's largest corporate self-learning platform.

A Mechanical Engineer from BITS Pilani, Management Graduate from XIM Bhubaneswar and Ph D in Management from Amity University, Dr. Mohapatra's illustrious corporate career spans over three and half decades. His tenure as Managing Director of IndianOil (Mauritius) Ltd. saw him turn the company into one of the top ten in the nation. As Chairman of Lanka IOC for nearly five years, he placed the company in the minds and hearts of people of Sri Lanka, particularly during the Lankan crisis.

A passionate advocate for education and inclusivity, he spearheaded CSR initiatives like Vidushi and IndianOil Shakti and chaired the Skill Development Institute in Bhubaneswar, creating a state of the art campus. His leadership during the pandemic earned him the Pride of India award for his compassionate approach to crisis management.

Bestowed with the HR Leader of the Year by *Economic Times*, an Honaris Causa from Manav Rachna Institute of International Research and Studies and a Distinguished Alumni of BITS Pilani, Dr. Mohapatra's work embodies the power of possibilities. His debut book offers a fresh perspective, blending heart and strategy to inspire leaders towards creating meaningful impact.